Rethinking the Sex Offender Registry Relative to Parole and Recidivism

Originally submitted by Kathy E. Williams as final project for Master of Science in Strategic Management from Indiana Wesleyan University (2012, December)

Published by Dr. Kathy E. Williams

Contents

Foreword

The contents of this report were originally submitted as my final project in completion of a Master's of Science in Strategic Management with Indiana Wesleyan University. It was completed in 2013, and I am writing this foreword in 2017. Although I obtained all necessary approvals during the writing of the paper and have those on file, any reference to the specific facility where I am employed has been changed to (the facility) and to the privatized corporation that oversees the facility as (the corporation). That replacement will serve as a benefit to the reader who can more easily generalize the content to any facility versus a specific location. Most of the information submitted in the work could be accessed by any individual from public resources. After submitting my project proposal, I said to the Assistant Superintendent of Reentry and Programs, "I don't know what I was thinking. I am just a chaplain." She immediately corrected me and said, "You are not JUST a chaplain. You are a corrections professional." Those words became the driving force for my willingness to take on such a complex and potentially volatile topic. There are volumes that could be written concerning the original intentions of establishing a sex offender registry along with identifying current flaws and possible amendments to that legislation.

I recognize that in this political society of ours, some will read about a privatized facility and immediately have a negative impression. For those persons, I sincerely wish that there was an opportunity to visit our facility. I often say, "WalMart (an example) wants to be the best at what they do so that they can be a leader in their field. It is the same with (the corporation)." The (the corporation) wants to be the best at what they do which gives those of us who staff the facilities tremendous leeway to submit proposals for programming. I am surrounded by visionary people, and we collectively strive to bring a true correctional environment to the men who are incarcerated. Those men are given every opportunity to receive the tools for healthy living, yet we do not lose sight that there is consistently room for improvement.

As I review this paper four years after its writing, there is nothing in the overall content that I would change. Obviously, achieving a Doctorate of Strategic Leadership from Regent University has equipped me more thoroughly to research, write programs, and serve as a consultant. I did not complete my MSM and put it on the shelf. This project became the spark for initiatives and not merely a document to fulfill degree requirements. Our chapel has initiated programs that contribute to the men's spiritual, religious, and moral development. My supervisor and I are deep into a project that has taken over a year to accumulate the data to address the most common parole violations discovered by this work. We are using that data to develop both interventive and preventive programming. Some of the questions that I have since postured and completed preliminary review toward developing research projects include:

- Reviewing the men over the age of 60 who have no prior criminal history. What happened in life that a sexual crime became an option? The results of that study could assist in developing preventive programming for our senior citizen males.
- Searching the question from a religious perspective, "Are there relative trends between particular religious groups and certain crimes?" The intention of the question is to delve into what sorts of beliefs and principles give a man resolution about such a complex crime? More specifically, I have prayerfully asked in my time as a chaplain, "God, what broke in a man's soul such that sexual crime became a viable outlet?"

The flame of my own commitment and that of my colleagues continues to burn brightly and there is intense commitment to bring opportunity for positive change into the lives of those who are incarcerated for sexual offenses. Nothing about this work is meant to diminish the tragic effects that sexual crime has on the victim nor to lessen accountability for the offender.

Dr. Kathy E. Williams

CASE DESCRIPTION
Introduction

Every stakeholder that is connected to the issue of sexual offenses unilaterally agrees that the registry, parole stipulations, and recidivism contain systemic challenges. Research within these areas remains in its infancy with policy makers, treatment providers, and vested agencies yet there is a fundamental need for evidence-based practices that can guide their efforts to more thoroughly secure public safety while simultaneously attempting to address a population of offenders that are as diverse as this nation's population. Although complex, the relationship between the sex offender registry and notification (SORN) requirements, parole stipulations, and the recidivism rate for the State of Indiana begs the question, "Are the registry requirements and parole stipulations combined causing a falsely inflated recidivism rate for the Indiana Department of Corrections?"

This case study is constructed on the basis of responding "Yes" to the above question which lends it to examine sex offender registry laws in the United States, historical and current developments in research, as well as policies and practices. The author has comprised an array of studies, personal interviews, primary research that will offer a snapshot of one particular population of sexual offenders, and principles of strategic management drawn from textbooks used throughout the Masters of Business Program with Indiana Wesleyan University. Recommendations will include privatization with specific consideration to (the corporation), joint venture options, and technological innovation while rethinking registry specifications and parole requirements. The conclusions will propose means of comprehensive supervision and effective reentry strategies for sex offenders filtered through management and economic considerations without compromising the public need for safety.

Purpose of the Study

This case study will investigate the past and current practices regarding sex offenders and propose additional considerations to assist in increasing successful reentry such that the number of individuals returning to incarceration due to technical violations of parole is reduced. The case will examine whether the registry and notification have proven to be effective in reducing recidivism among sex offenders and will consider obtainable alternative techniques and practices to current parole procedures. It is beyond the scope of this project to offer an exhaustive review of national or state efforts in this area simply due to restraints with time and quantity of materials available; however, it is expected that the conclusions offered will enhance and, to some degree, challenge already existing works in this field of study. There are gaps of data that will be identified and might conceivably become the subject of further research.

Significance of the Study

The audience for this case study includes victims and their network of family and acquaintances, community stakeholders, policymakers, service providers, researchers, and sex offenders. In part, the process of this study will challenge the "fear factor" of public perception and the legislative process by which, ". . . SORN laws became the norm without any systemic study of their consequences (Prescott, p. 48)." The challenge is not intended to dismiss the impact of sexual offenses nor will it discount the collateral consequences brought about by sexual crimes. Nevertheless, the study will spotlight logical problems with policies and practices. Examining and separating recidivism for new crimes versus recidivism for technical violations on parole will aid us in outlining the effectiveness (or not) of the registry and our need to rethink its purpose. This case study is significant as it opens discussion of ". . . the 'elephant in the living room' that has quelled the successful implementation of policies and programs founded on good research and/or sound theory (Paparozzi & Guy, p. 401)."

Significance to the Writer

As a chaplain with the (the facility) which houses a majority population of male sex offenders, the countless interactions have inspired an interest for this writer to question what is needed for the offenders to reenter society as productive citizens rather than at-risk individuals living on borrowed time that will likely be shortened by technical violations of parole. Institutionalizing individuals through repeated returns to a penal facility is not in the best interests of our society (which includes all parties involved in this case study). Being employed in one of two privatized facilities within the Indiana Department of Corrections has educated this writer to appreciate the efficiency and thoroughness of services that can be provided through privatization, particularly with consideration to (the corporation). That combination of interest has raised intriguing possibilities that do not demean other studies or practices but build on them to move toward innovative standards for best practices in this field.

Significance to Stakeholders

The stakeholders for this case study rest along a continuum that includes the victim and those related to their lives as well as the offender and those relative to their lives (many times a crossover group), systems providers (law enforcement, judicial, correctional, and others), policymakers, community, and others either primarily or secondarily impacted by sexual crime. It is an essential discussion for stakeholders to question whether Megan's Law, the Jacob Wetterling Act, or the Adam Walsh Protection Act (AWA) and its components such as the Sex Offender Registry and Notification Act (SORN) have proven to be deterrents for sexual crime.

8

"On the surface, they have intuitive appeal. However, intuition is not science, and a closer look at the laws' purpose, intent, and outcomes reveals that problems do exist (Bonnar-Kidd, p. 413)." Current laws and practices are not to be disregarded; however, there is room to refine partnerships and offer an additional lens for viewing efficacy and implementing revisions as needed.

The Indiana Department of Corrections (hereafter referred to as IDOC) is a primary stakeholder which compels a discussion of their role in impacting recidivism rates as well as the light that is cast on them (fairly or not which will be part of our later discussion) through the high rates of technical violations by those individuals on parole. IDOC has a capacity of nearly 30,000 adult offenders (IDOC 2011 Annual Report). Another major stakeholder is (the corporation) who presently contracts with IDOC at the Plainfield Short Term Offender Program (Hereafter referred to as S.T.O.P.) Facility and the (the facility). A third major stakeholder is the Parole Services Division of IDOC who has approximately 18,000 offenders on its caseload at any time (Indiana Parole, 2012). A discussion of each of those entities in this case study will include economic considerations, policy implications, change implementation theories, critical thinking-based initiatives, and a SWOT (strengths, weaknesses, opportunities, and threats) analysis of their capability to incorporate evidence-based practices into their environment.

The clear first stakeholder is the victim. While aggregate repercussions to this group cannot be addressed within the scope of this case study, attention will be given to their perceptions of sex offenders and the dangers those individuals characterize to the victims and their community of family, neighbors, etc. The push to categorize sexual offenses as a public health concern has at least one strong implication – education. Statistics uniformly prove that most sexual crimes are committed as "close" or "near" crimes rather than "stranger" crimes which increases an inquiry concerning fewer sexual crimes due to the registry or fewer reported crimes due to issues of shame and embarrassment on the part of the victim (Prescott, 2012). For victims, this case study will clarify numerous challenges while simultaneously offering the hope of accuracies and effective best practices.

Broader Implications

Broader implications extend throughout the United States. "Criminal recidivism generates significant social harm (Prescott, p. 48)." While most will agree with the previous statement, the methods used to deter or correct that social harm remains under scrutiny. One area that must be examined is the, ". . . significant economic costs associated with sex offender registration and notification, which produce little or no increase in public safety (Tewksbury, Jennings, & Zgoba, p. 22)." The collateral consequences to the community extend even to property values where a 2011 study shows, ". . . homes close to a registered offender sell for about $5,500 less than comparable homes (Agan, p. 207)." Sex offender registration is managed at a local level; however, there are now federal minimum standards for registration and notification. The bureaucracy of the systems involved has a propensity toward seeming like a relay team unsure whether to pass the baton to the runner in front or to the runner in the back rather than smoothly passing the baton forward with a goal of completing the course.

One of the more extensive outcomes from this case study is the demonstration of the lack of conclusive research to support furthering or the use of registry and notification procedures. For much of the campaign to enact registry, "The premise was, and still is, that with this knowledge, citizens will take protective measures against the nearby sex offenders (Zgoba, Witt, Dalessandro, & Veysey 2008)." Despite prevalent community support for these laws, there is minimal substantial evidence to support their effectiveness in reducing either first-time offenses or re-offenses. Broadening the scope of assessment tools to measure both, ". . . criminal thought process (how an offender thinks) with . . . a measure of criminal thought content (what an offender thinks) (Walters, p. 218)" is necessary to achieve a more comprehensive view of sexual offenders and effective remedies for their conduct.

To suitably administrate essential alternations to current systems, this case study includes change implementation theories, critical thinking skills, organizational change, and principles of strategic management combined with ethical guidance and dynamic leadership models. Examining the strengths and weaknesses of current practices through a management model will neutralize the emotional public attachment to the issue and step away from the media practices of highlighting the most horrific cases as the norm. With a factual and practical approach, we will rethink how the sex offender registry is attached to parole stipulations and the subsequent impact on recidivism rates. The recommendations and conclusions offered are not designed to take away from previous efforts but are offered to add thoroughness and clarity as tools to improve public safety as well as successful reentry for those convicted of sexual offenses.

Organizational Overview

The organizational overview for this case study involves IDOC, (the corporation), and the Parole Services Division. "The comparison of strengths, weaknesses, opportunities, and threats is normally referred to as a SWOT analysis (Hill & Jones, p. 19)." A SWOT analysis aligns company resources and competencies to the business environment in which it functions. The SWOT analysis lays the foundation for the strategies to be used in a particular industry or field. For the three organizations cited, there are comparable strengths, weaknesses, opportunities, and threats as displayed in Figure 1.

Figure 1 - *SWOT Analysis of IDOC, (the corporation), and Parole Services Division*

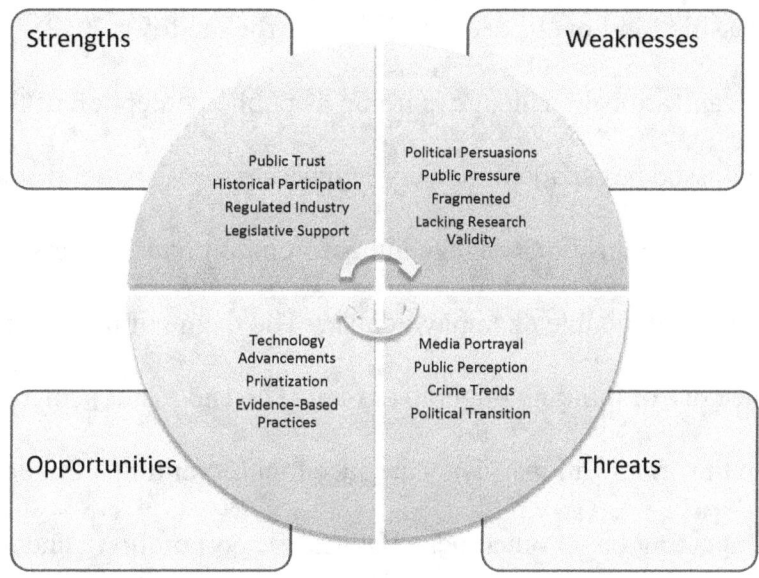

The Indiana State Prison opened its doors in October 1822 in Jeffersonville, IN where

prisoners were confined to hard labor (Friends of Indiana State Archives, 2012). Total costs for

the land was little more than $4,000. 190 years and 1 month later, that amount of money cannot

sustain the expense of one inmate for more than a slight portion of a year. IDOC currently

consists of 20 adult and 5 juvenile facilities (Overview of adult and juvenile facilities, 2012).

The term parole comes from a French word that means giving one's word of honor. It reflects

the Middle Ages where prisoners would give their word to abide by certain rules if they were

permitted an early release. Parole has been in effect in the United States since Civil War times

(Parole Historical Roots, 2012). Indiana's Parole Division includes eight districts with the

largest population served in Indianapolis. (the corporation) is the youngest of the three

organizations having its beginning in 1984. (the corporation) is a world leader in privatized

correction and detention facilities with operations in the United States, Australia, South Africa,

and the United Kingdom. Its largest privatized facility in the U.S. is located in the Midwest with

a recent expansion to include a 512-bed maximum security facility bringing the total inmates housed at that site to 3,196; however, the primary population of sex offenders is housed within the 2,500 that are classified in Level 2 security housing (the facility), 2012).

Part of the organizational challenge is ironic as public perception of the severity of sexual offenses as a criminal issue has sparked the very legislation that is under discussion, yet the same public perception of the organizations engaged in enforcing the rules seems to be one of accepting the outcome as inevitable and unavoidable. The theme of being "tough on crime" has become a single trajectory of thinking – lock them up. The end result is that change thinking has to come from within the organizations. They are faced with pointing a finger at their own performance and demanding better outcomes. IDOC, (the corporation), and Parole have the capabilities of raising the bar, resetting goals and objectives, revising policies and practices, and achieving the excellence required to successfully meet their first objective of public safety while effectively assisting convicted individuals to successfully break the cycle of recidivism and become a useful member of the community.

Identification and Discussion of Issues

In the technology-driven world of our modern age and the vigorous campaign of upward mobility in the workforce, the parameters placed on sex offenders literally drive them back to an age that few of us could even consider. The simplest day-to-day movements of the average citizen become a figurative chess game for sex offenders. Most would think nothing of passing a child in an aisle at Wal-Mart or at church or while taking a walk in our neighborhood, but for a sex offender, that situation becomes a reportable "incidental" contact with their parole officer with the potential for a polygraph to test the sincerity of their reporting. "The potential longstanding consequences of sex crimes for victims, combined with the public's fear of these offenders, intense media and public scrutiny, and special laws designed to restrict sex offender's movement and behavior create significant challenges for paroling authorities . . . (Thigpen, Beauclair, Keiser, & Banks, p. 1)." Those same stipulations create a maze for offenders to conquer in order to achieve any sort of normalcy for their existence.

Interpreting data is an ongoing task. ". . . clinicians are prone to err on the side of caution (e.g. hospitalizing a patient who describes thoughts of self-harm even though the actuarial risk is low) (Bani-Yaghoub, et al, p. 349)." The problem plays into the misconstructions of public ideology that sex offenders are a homogenous group that can be handled as a "one size fits all" risk group that cannot and do not change. The (the facility), with over 90% of its population serving time for sexual crimes, currently uses the Indiana Risk Assessment System (hereafter referred to as IRAS). A snapshot of the assessment is offered in Figure 2[1].

Figure 2 - *Indiana Risk Assessment System (IRAS) Summary*

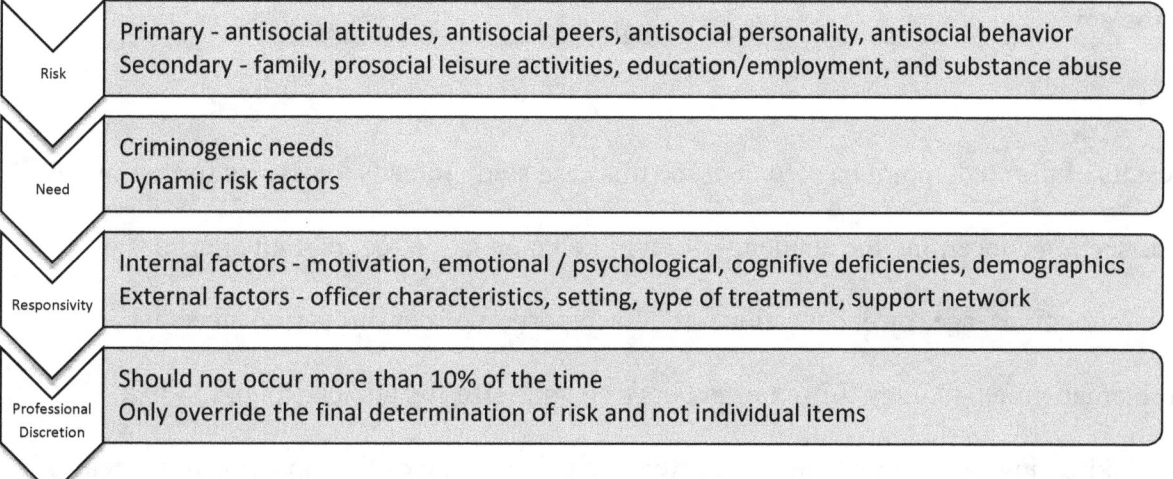

"The Sex Offender Treatment Intervention and Progress Scale (SOTIPS) is a statistically-driven dynamic measure designed to aid clinicians, correctional caseworkers, and probation and parole officers in assessing risk, treatment, and supervision needs, and progress among adult males who have been convicted of

---

[1] Information Retrieved from The Indiana Risk Assessment System published by University of Cincinnati

one or more qualifying sexual offenses and committed at least one of these sexual

offenses after their 18th birthday (McGrath, Cumming, & Lasher, p. 1)."

The SOTIPS offers one of the most recently revised strategies, including a sample of 759

adult male sex offenders who were enrolled in community treatment program between 2001 and

2007. Figure 3 charts a progression of the 14 risk items[2] used in the SOTIPS evaluation.

Figure 3 - *Sex Offender Treatment Intervention and Progress Scale (SOTIPS) Risk Items*

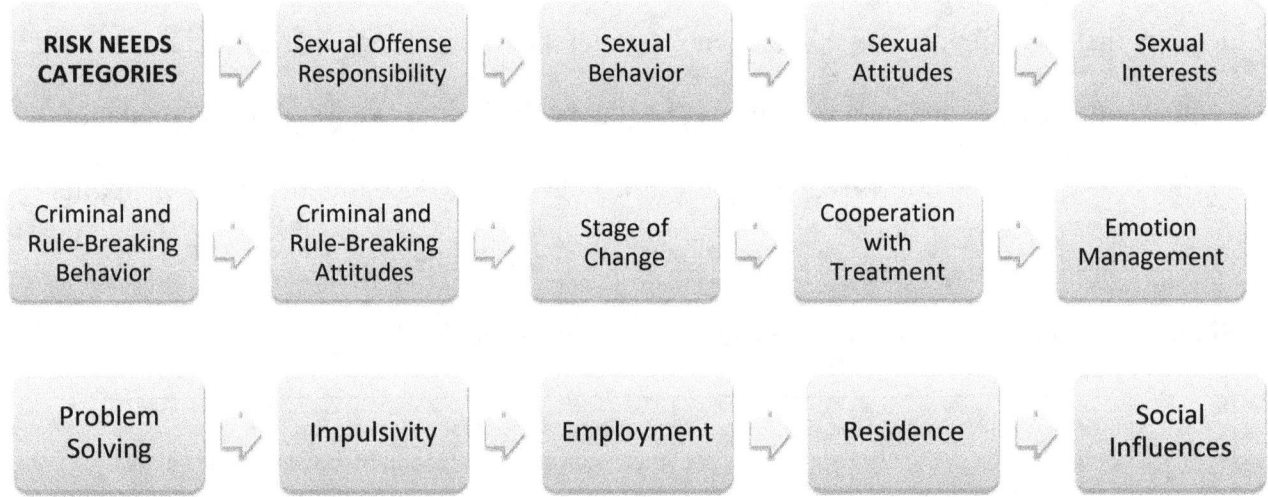

The results of the study point back to an issue this case study intends to discuss further in the

analysis section concerning the challenges of a mixed population, i.e. particular crimes or

technical violations, age, race, education, etc. Each portion of our discussion steers us back to

the problematic methodology for sex offenders as a "one size fits all" endeavor.

Addressing issues concerning sex offenders is likely one of the most sensitive areas of

public concern in our nation. "Although sex offenders account for only a small percentage of the

total offender population, probably no other group of offenders evokes as much fear in citizens

and concern among policymakers and practitioners (Enhancing the Management of Adult and

---

[2] Retrieved from SOTIPS: Sex Offender Treatment Intervention and Progress Scale (2012) published by McGrath, Robert J., Cumming, (the corporation)rgia, P., & Lasher, Michael P.

Juvenile Sex Offenders, p. 3)." Appendix A encapsulates two manuals offered by the Center for Sex Offender Management that are designed for policymakers and practitioners.

One of the most significant challenges across the board is the need for collaboration. The Center for Sex Offender Management (CSOM) offers a simplistic model that is crucial to forming policies and determining practices. Figure 4 demonstrates the four-step process recommended by CSOM.[3]

Figure 4 - *Center for Sex Offender Management Model for Policies and Practices*

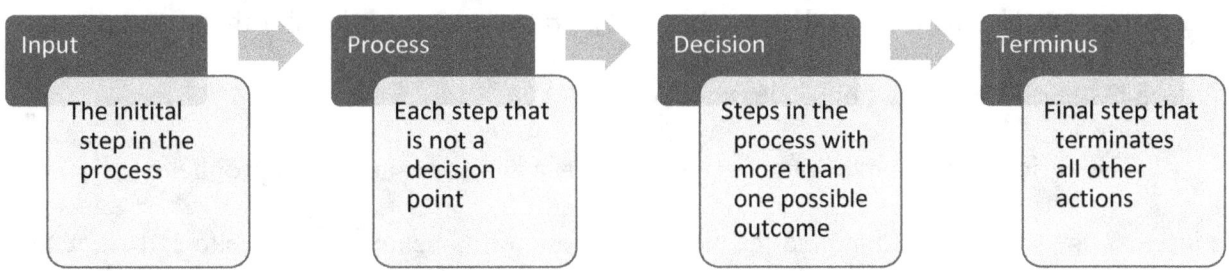

The two major players in this case study include IDOC and the Parole Supervision Division. Beginning with IDOC, we note the following statement, "We do not like hospitals that do not cure or schools that do not educate. And we should not like prisons that do not rehabilitate (Cullen, Johnson, & Eck, p. 78)." The follow-up services to incarceration begin when an individual is released to parole. This case study is primarily concerned with technical violations which typically include an offender's failure,

> ". . . to (a) comply with curfews, (b) pass alcohol and drug urinalysis screens, (c) avoid contact with other offenders, (d) maintain employment and/or report unemployment, (e) attention meetings with probation and parole officers (PPOs), (f) make restitution payments and/or perform community service hours, and (g) attend individual or group therapy meetings (Kerbs, Jones & Jolley, p. 425)."

---

[3] Retrieved from Enhancing the Management of Adult and Juvenile Sex Offenders: A Handbook for Policymakers and Practitioners published by Center for Sex Offender Management

As of January 1, 2012, IDOC had 9,529 adult males on parole and 1,128 adult females on parole (Offender Population Statistical Report, (b). Of those totals, 2,241 adult males were supervised by Parole District #3 which is Indianapolis. Monthly returns to prison due to technical violations for 2011 total 127 male offenders and 13 female offenders while total releases to parole were 644 male offenders and 82 female offenders (Offender Population Statistical Report, p. 9). Appendix B includes a summation chart of the total number of felony offenses committed to IDOC during 2011 such that it shows only sexual crimes and no other felony offenses. The majority of that number will be released on parole after the offender has achieved his/her Earliest Possible Release Date (EPRD).

"The variable that marks some periods as barren and some as rich in prophetic vision is in the interest, the level of seeking, and the responsiveness of the hearers. It is seekers, then, who make the prophet . . . (Greenleaf, p. 10)." While it may seem initially strange to insert a comment about prophetic vision, the reader is encouraged to reconsider the numerous studies that weave a common thread of agreement – there is a need to rethink the sex offender registry in regards to parole stipulations and how technical violations impact recidivism. The hearers, in this situation, include the general public and their perceptions. If we can transition the term prophet to also mean leader, then we may go further into Robert Greenleaf's writings when he says we can become ". . . affirmative builders of a better society (p. 12)." His work, *The Servant as Leader*, is highly recommended as a guideline to achieving the needed organizational changes in order to better accomplish the primary goals of corrections, which is public safety.

SCOM's report, *Legislative Trends in Sex Offender Management,* demonstrates a four-fold burden carried by sex offender laws illustrated in Figure 5[4].

---

[4] Retrieved from Legislative Trends in Sex Offender Management published by Center for Sex Offender Management

Figure 5 - *Four-fold Burden of Sex-Offender Specific Laws*

Incapacitation

Confining sex offenders either by criminal or civil commitment.

Retribution / Punishment

Delivering punishment or sanctions proportional to the severity of the crime.

Deterrence

Threatening a response or sanction severe enough to cause restraint.

Rehabiliation

Providing treatment or intervention designed to address sex offending.

Much of the support for harsher laws and lengthy sentences is the opinion of the public that examples can be made of those already convicted such that it will deter other individuals from committing similar crimes. The increasingly higher rates of incarceration strain state budgets and divert financial support away from community-based programs and resources making for a complex and yet unanswered question about which platform can more effectively address the four-fold burden previously listed.

Questions to be Answered

In this case study, we will consider the implications of the Sex Offender Registry and Notification Act (SORNA) requirements as they relate to individuals on parole and their combined influence on recidivism rates for the Indiana Department of Corrections.

Is there a societal benefit in rethinking the sex offender registry from the intent of its original function as it applies to parole stipulations for released sex offenders?

This case study will offer a detailed history of sex offender laws in the analysis section. For purposes of a generalized response to the stated question, we revert to the discussion of differentiating between public perception and statistical truth. Nothing about this case study is intended to remove accountability or to promote tolerance for a sexual crime. The concept of rethinking the implications of a registry relative to parole stipulations is in hopes of promoting a less bureaucratically entangled and more streamlined and thorough means of accomplishing the tasks of supervision and accountability combined with the goals of progressive reentry for those offenders. The question posed will hopefully uncover deficiencies but not without offering resolutions. The analysis is not designed as a faultfinding exploration but to enhance systems already in place.

The average thinking route includes a multi-level experience. Level 1 is an observable event that is then perceived through emotions and feelings such that Level 2 is the unobservable conclusion (internal about ourselves and external about others) that is drawn based on our Level 3 thinking which incorporates values, assumptions, beliefs, and expectations (VABEs). "Unless we understand the core VABEs of people, we are not likely to be successful in guiding them through a change process (Clawson, p. 167)." To propose any rethinking of the sex offender registry will necessitate finding a way to fulfill the expectations of a nation fashioned in diversity with a population of over 300 million citizens. Using the principles of critical mass, this case study does not propose to be the total solution but is respectfully bringing input that along with many others will compel a new result or action to occur.

As we consider the question concerning recidivism, there are two major schools of thought. One teaches that almost 40 percent of offenders will recidivate and, more explicitly, that almost 70 percent of sex offenders will recidivate. The second states that only 1.05 percent of sex offenders will return to prison for a new sexual crime. With such a massive gap in the statistical citations concerning sex offenders, we are compelled to ask what is at stake for citing one or the other. Who benefits from the first set of extremely high returns (or the second)? One question continues to stir another and another. What sorts of parole violations tend to dominate those who are ordered returned to a correctional facility? IDOC is an award-winning system; therefore, it is all the more critical that the agency is cast in the best possible light to reflect its progressive programming and success stories. Examining the stated question will help to continue forward in that trend.

Methodologies

Innate sociocentrism says, "It's true because we believe it" which worded another way, "I assume that the dominant beliefs with the groups to which I belong are true even though I have never questioned the basis for these beliefs (Paul & Elder, p. 215)." Multiple studies offer conclusions that differ from the average citizen's "truth" about sex offenders. The mind has three realms of thinking – thoughts, feelings, and desires. Sociocentric thinking includes the natural tendency to discard evidence and align with what is most appeasing to the two-thirds of our thinking that is feelings and desires. A critical thinking process overcomes our sociocentric processing and carefully seeks evidence and information that may invert our natural tendency to disregard. In order to enter a discussion of something as sensitive as sexual offenses, we must collectively engage in critical thinking processes. Initial reactions to suggested changes likely will gain a response of, "That will never work" but this case study's intention is to outline options that will take precedence over the sociocentric mind with critical thinking practices.

This case study will examine data from the Indiana Department of Corrections and more specifically, the (the facility) to pinpoint the primary technical violations that return individuals to incarceration and offer alternative responses for those events. The writer will include interviews with corrections and parole professionals with many years of experience who can speak knowledgeably concerning system gaps, working strategies, and suggested revisions. Reviews and recommendations from scholarly literature and field journals will provide a baseline of discussion. Whether we choose to view him from a biblical or a historical lens, the Maxwell Leadership Bible defines Nehemiah as a 360-degree leader. His leadership sequence was to lead himself with discipline and responsibility, lead the king he served with excellence and respect, lead his countrymen with service and perspective, and lead as governor with vision, integrity, and planning (Maxwell & Elmore, 2007). This case study strives to operate in the principles of those 360 degrees of leadership.

CASE SOLUTION
Information and Literature Review

The primary focus of this paper deals with Indiana Sex Offender Registry and parole stipulations relative to the Indiana Department of Corrections (IDOC) recidivism rates. The case study will examine whether parole stipulations for sex offenders have caused an excessive number of technical violations that are inflating IDOC recidivism; therefore, the result will examine whether there is a need to rethink the sex offender registry stipulations and parole stipulations. Current authorities agree that this is an area of research in its infancy as sex offender registries have largely existed only since 1991. Research offers a continuum of insights, including therapeutic prisons, the validity of the registry (or not), parole decision making, and the goals and objectives of the registry.

The Information and Literature Review contains sixty resources that are relevant to the case study discussion by offering a synopsis of each resource.

Overview / Background of the Sexual Offender Laws and the Sex Offender Registry

As the case study develops, it is essential to note the beginnings of legislative, legal, and criminal justice initiatives for the nation. The initial sex offender law in the United States was implemented in California in 1947; however, it was not until the mid-1990's that the nation as a whole began to implement registries. Since that time, there is an ongoing need to examine sex offenders reentering communities balanced against public perception and fear of "stranger danger." Legislative efforts have largely been in response to high media profile cases that may not reflect an accurate depiction of sexual crimes and their consequences to society. (Grubesic & Murray, 2009). Sex crimes are considered to be a seriously underreported crime due to factors of fear, shame, guilt, blame, and embarrassment by the victim. The greatest challenge to law enforcement is that there is no common portrait of a sex offender as they come from all socio-economic, educational, and cultural backgrounds (CSOM Fact Sheet: What You Need to Know About Sex Offenders, 2012).

Recent trends are striving to define sexual offenses as a public health problem rather than merely a criminal justice issue. The Jacob Wetterling Crimes Against Children Act of 1994, Megan's Law of 1996, and the Adam Walsh Protection Act (AWA) of 2007 combine as the crux of sex offender laws in the United States (Bonnar-Kidd, 2010). Megan's Laws is a collective set of legislation concerning community registration and notification. The goal of notification is primarily to alert past victims as well as the community although minimal research has been conducted to verify whether the existence of such laws has proven to be effective for either reduction of new crime or prevention of recidivism (Zgoba, et al., 2008).

State of Indiana Code 11-8-8 sets forth requirements concerning the Indiana Sex and Violent Offender Registry. Following lawsuits by *Richard P. Wallace v. State of Indiana* and *Todd Jensen v. State of Indiana*, the Indiana Supreme Court ruled that it is unconstitutional for individuals who committed certain sexual crimes prior to July 1, 2007 to be required to register unless there have been additional sexual crimes beyond that date. The Indiana Department of Corrections was appointed to oversee the Registry as of July 1, 2006 (Sex & Violent Offender Registry, 2012). "Recently . . . in *Bond vs. U.S.*, the Supreme Court has granted standing for sex offenders to challenge SORNA on 10th Amendment grounds, where previously they had no standing to do so (Sex Offender Registration and Notification in the United States: Current Case Law and Issues, p. 7)." Several matters of case law have addressed retroactive application and ex post facto issues with sex offenders and the registry. Other arguments are based on " . . .

double jeopardy, procedural due process, substantive due process, equal protection, ineffective assistance of counsel, the Sixth Amendment right to trial by jury, cruel and unusual punishment, full faith & credit, the supremacy clause, and separation of powers (Sex Offender Registration and Notification in the United States: Current Case Law and Issues, p. 7)."

Organizational Contributors

The sex offender registration laws and sex offender notification laws are twin appendages to the judicial and correctional systems that remain largely unproven as effective in actually making the public safe. Once released from serving their sentence in the correctional system, most individuals are placed on either parole (guided by the state) or probation (guided by the county) for a fixed period of time. Much of the current research advocates that parole stipulations enforcing the registry and notification laws promote recidivism, "crime displacement," and mistakenly promote awareness as a detection tool (Prescott, 2012). As a result, recidivism rates are inflated with technical violations, i.e. failure to secure an approved address, failure to pay required fees, urine tests proving positive for drugs, etc.

The review of articles for this case study includes some with fundamental information that will support various sections with historical and organizational data. Included in those pieces are the simple count of facilities within IDOC, which includes twenty adult and five juvenile facilities (Overview of Adult and Juvenile Facilities, 2012). As of January 1, 2012, the total population within IDOC included 25,666 adult male offenders and 2,385 adult female offenders (Offender Population Statistics, 2011). Site-specific within those adult facilities is the (the facility) which houses a 90 percent (plus) population of sexual offenders (the facility) / (the corporation), 2012). The organizational aspect of the case study begins with a historical view of IDOC and its first adult facility constructed in Jeffersonville, IN in 1822 (More than Dillinger,

2012). Parole has been in use within the State of Indiana since the Civil War and has its origins in Medieval Times when a man's word was his bond of honor that if released, he would live as a law-abiding citizen (Parole Historical Roots, 2012).

Evidence-based practices (EBP) lay a foundation for correctional professionals to examine what works and what does not or has not worked. One area of scrutiny is prisoner reentry which happens through parole supervision. With prison and jail populations exploding by 500% in the past 30 years, correctional expenditures increasing by 660% between 1982 and 2006, and a 262% increase in parolees in the same period, discretionary parole practices is a tool that can intervene with historically poor planning practices by correctional systems (Paparozzi & Guy, 2009). Change implementation theory is a strategic piece to addressing the planning challenges facing not only the system actors but the external stakeholders of the general public. Developing a shared diagnosis is crucial as, "Diagnosis is meant to create learning about the real, current, and unique dynamics . . . combined with mutual engagement, it is designed to create deep and wide commitment to the desired outcome (Spector, 2010, p. 59)."

Evidence-based practices will steer the correctional industry away from practices that are primarily rooted in fears generated by the media and public perception and toward critical thinking that operates from the rational mind. The goals and objectives will address sociocentric thinking through conceptual analysis and ideologies while supporting the public need to feel safe (Paul & Elder, 2006). A principle actor in this process is (the corporation) as a provider for a continuum of care services. The company's recent acquisition of an auxiliary company and its electronic monitoring capabilities has positioned (the corporation) to participate in necessary change implementation and conversion to critical thinking in regards to parole practices (the corporation) Annual Report, 2011).

The Indiana Department of Corrections presently has approximately 18,000 offenders under the supervision of its parole agents. The Department facilitates a Re-entry Accountability Plan (RAP) as soon as an individual is assigned to a corrections facility with the goal of preparing that person for coming back to their community. There are five acting members of the Indiana Parole Board appointed by the Governor to serve four-year terms (Indiana Parole, 2012). IDOC Commissioner Bruce Lemmon offered the following encouragement, ". . . we achieved the highest honor with the American Correctional Association (ACA) by earning the Golden Eagle Award, shown a reduction in the rate of recidivism for adult offenders, and expanded utilization of Community Corrections to help divert lower-risk defendants from prison (IDOC Annual Report, p. 5)." Unfortunately, the definition of recidivism is not a stable definition as it fluctuates from one agency to another. For purposes of IDOC, recidivism is defined as, ". . . return to incarceration within three years of the offender's date of release (IDOC Adult Recidivism Rates, 2012)."

Reorganizing entire components of our legislative statutes relative to corrections and parole supervision is a significant undertaking that must include the principles of Lewin's field theory in social science. His three stages of change implementation – unfreezing, moving, and refreezing – provide a systematic process of change implementation, although most effective change will be achieved by incorporating other dynamics such as gaining the public confidence in shared diagnosis and mutual engagement (Spector, B., 2010). Added to the challenges in organizing for assessment and proposal for change are the multiple political forces at work which leads us toward examining the body of research through the eyes of Robbins & Judge and their influence tactics (Robbins & Judge, 2010).

Any effort to address organizational concerns must first be processed through the lens of the Sex and Violent Offender Registration Responsibilities as listed under Indiana Code (IC) 11-8-8-8 and compliant with the Sex and Violent Offender Registry under Indiana Code (IC) 36-2-13-5.5. Each stipulated definition is attached to a specific Indiana Code and is listed beside the criminal statute (Sex and Violent Offender Registration Responsibilities and Other Duties, 2012). Research about the static and dynamic factors for criminal recidivism is based in variables such as triggers and lifestyle stability. Those notions challenge the current goals of the sex offender registry and its implications to parole supervision and must be included in any worthwhile discussion of recidivism (Brown, St. Amand, & Zambie, 2008).

A complex alignment is that of the public perception concerning sex offenders which is largely based on media presentation of a few highly publicized crimes versus the actuality of legislature's primary interests and objectives which include incapacitation, retribution/punishment, deterrence, and rehabilitation (Legislative trends in sex offender management, 2008). Prisons are attached to a paradoxical view that their role is to keep "the new dangerous class" segregated from society while simultaneously preparing them for successful reentry to a society that demands continued segregation after release. Despite its known iatrogenic effects and more sticks than carrots approach, particular schools of research call for a transformation of prisons to become institutions of accountability. A general consensus that can be posed is that, ". . . prisons have largely failed to reduce offender recidivism (Cullen, Johnson, & Eck, 2012, p. 77)."

Alongside the model for accountability is the proposition for therapeutic prisons. Based on the premise of capacity and content across eight recognized domains, this model is heavily dependent on organizational harmony for policies and procedures that sustain program delivery

(Smith & Schweitzer, 2012). Piloting new directions in any industry command a need for competitive advantage, strategic domains, a recognized value chain, core capabilities, and the essential elements of strategic thinking. Leadership that is grounded in strategy is an absolute for the complexities facing innovative practice demands (Clawson, 2009). Accountability and therapeutic approaches to an issue deemed a public health crisis will most effectively be delivered by those who can see themselves as servant leaders. Incorporating leadership by persuasion brings the fruit of conviction rather than cooperation by coercion. Intuition and foresight, acceptance and empathy, awareness and perception, and healing and serving are woven together to effectively secure community in all aspects (Greenleaf, 2008).

Examination of efforts to reduce recidivism unavoidably takes us to the area of education. Despite strong correlations between educational achievement and reduced recidivism, Indiana made the choice in the spring of 2011 to severely slash any funding for education within prisons. "Effective July 1, 2011, the State Student Assistance Commission of Indiana is prohibited from awarding grants to a "confined felon" (Loughlin, 2011)." The study titled, "Managing the Challenges of the Sex Offender Registry" (2007) contains an entire phase called, "Reach Out" which includes educational training and vocational services as crucial increments of the transition plan for offenders. A 5-year longitudinal study of 6,561 offenders released from IDOC resulted in a conclusion that, ". . . an offender's education has a simultaneous effect on both post-release employment and recidivism (Nally, Lockwood, Ho, & Knutson, p. 23)."

A leading technology that has recently been employed is the use of electronic monitoring technology. Since 2006, 22 states have passed legislation authorizing some form of Global Positioning Satellite (GPS) for tracking sex offenders. The four benefits most widely noted by using this technology are flexibility, reintegration, control, and investigation, although this area of monitoring lacks any substantial evidence-based research. Complications yet to be addressed include a false sense of security, legal issues, limitations, and the need to clarify goals and objectives (International Association of Police Chiefs, 2008). Industry buzzwords such as collaboration are many times theoretically sound but practically impotent. One group of stakeholders that must be seen as a viable partner in the practical engagement of community enforcement is the local police department. Inclusion of local police greatly assists with the exchange of information, coordinating resources, and offering a front-line confirmation of addresses and personal contact for sex offenders (Key Roles of Law Enforcement in Sex Offender Management, 2008).

The use of framing analysis provides schemata of interpretation that can enhance individual-, organizational-, and field-level outcomes for policies concerning parole supervision. By addressing frame alignment, there is a collective interpretive fit within organizations related to policies and practices concerning sex offenders. Using California's New Parole Model (NPM) as a pattern for best practices, states across the U.S. can process their efforts through four frames – principled, practical, authoritative, and materialist (Rudes, 2012). A three-tier research to explore whether the sex offender registry is relative to a decrease in sexual crime; whether sex offender registries reduce recidivism; and whether higher concentrations of sex offenders helps to predict the location of sexual abuse crimes results in questions concerning target hardening, disintegrative shaming, and opportunity costs for committing future crimes (Agan, 2011).

Recidivism refers to a return to prison within three years of the offender's date of release. Indiana presently has one of the lowest recidivism rates in the nation with new sexual offenses at 1.05% within 3 years of exiting a correctional facility. The return rates of nearly 70% for sexual offenders are typically for technical (noncriminal) violations such as residency restrictions or registration issues. Those numbers must assist us in directing public safety, legislative, and economic decision making toward renovating the system that oversees sexual offenders (Indiana's Recidivism Rates Decline for Third Consecutive Year, 2012). The U.S. incarcerates its citizens at the highest rate of any country in the world with an ever-increasing number incarcerated due to technical violations after their earliest possible release date (EPRD). Parole agents are given discretionary decision-making parameters which lend the situations to being addressed by personal judgment or discretion. The world of parole agents would benefit from aligning to a procedural policy that safeguards against issues (extralegal factors) that rest outside of an offender's past or present criminal conduct (legal factors) (Kerbs, Jones, & Jolley, 2009).

Directing a cleaner model of addressing sex offenders will streamline the multiplicity of overlapping systems currently in place. This phenomenon is called venue sorting which is the process of cases being interchanged from one organizational setting to another with each setting hosting its own culture and procedures. Addressing nested functions and parallel functions as building blocks to understanding more generalized theories is essential when addressing parole revocation (Lin, Grattet, & Petersilia, 2012).

Policymaker and Practitioner Issues

Many details that clarify policy issues stem from lawsuits filed by those affected most directly by legislation – sex offenders. *Jensen v. State*, 905 N.E.2d 384, 396-98, (Ind. 2009) resulted in a 4-1 ruling by the Indiana Supreme Court that, ". . . classifying a man a sexually violent predator . . . doesn't violate Indiana's prohibition of ex post facto laws or the doctrine of separation of powers (Nelson, 2011)." Erroneously labeling is the subject of *Thomas Andrews v. State of Indiana*, 29A02-1112-MI-1166 which resulted in the 7th Circuit Court ruling that there must be a broader discussion with all stakeholders and possible centralization of the administration of the registry (Stafford, 2012). In the case of *Patrick Fields v. Edwin G. Buss*, the plaintiff alleged that participation in the SOMMS program violated his constitutional rights regarding the Fifth Amendment, although the U.S. District Court Southern District of Indiana ultimately ruled that the self-incrimination clause applies only to evidence used during a criminal case and is not applicable to the program stipulations of self-disclosure (*Patrick Fields v. Edwin G. Buss,* 1:09-cv-00603-TWP-DML, 2011). *Michael Greer and John Maggi v. Edwin Buss, et al.* is a lawsuit filed against IDOC requiring 10-year registration periods from the perspective that the sex offender registry is a punitive action, particularly in the case of additional registration years added for new crimes beyond the initial 10-year period (Hoskins, 2010).

The Center for Sex Offender Management offers a detailed twenty-strategy guide built on collaborative case management and including specialized strategies for juvenile sex offenders along with state-specific proven programming that is an invaluable tool for policymakers and practitioners (Twenty Strategies for Advancing Sex Offender Management in Your Jurisdiction, 2008). After one generation of sex offender registry practices in the U.S., it is time to assess not only the intended goals and objectives concerning public safety but the unintended consequences such as the influences on deterring new crime and recidivism. In order to have clarity with its scope and comprehensive effectiveness, there must be multidisciplinary teams of stakeholders at local, state, and national levels (The Comprehensive Assessment Protocol: A Systemwide Review of Adult and Juvenile Sex Offender Management Strategies, 2007, p. 347). Research evidence does not support the belief that the sex offender registry better informs the public which, in turn, increases their safety from offenses. "There is a great diversity among sex offenders and corresponding recidivism rates when looking at their preference for victims (Tewksbury, Wesley, & Zgoba, p. 1)."

"Public notification systems negatively affect the stability and social reintegration of offenders in ways that the offender registration databases do not . . . (Sex Offender Registries and Notification Programs, 2009)" which leads lawmakers and law enforcement to establish clear distinctions between the two systems. Policy recommendations include the development of a comprehensive, multidisciplinary system for sex offender management based on five tactical goals that call for change and implementation strategies (Enhancing the Management of Adult and Juvenile Sex Offenders: A Handbook for Policymakers and Practitioners, 2007, p. 83). A more detailed investigation regarding recidivism is the research that measures criminal thought process (how an offender thinks) against criminal thought content (what an offender thinks) and their relativity to time, criminal thinking construct, and response styles (Walters, 2011).

Policy attention that is victim-centered with a public health focus must give consideration to the stakeholders involved with sex offender registry and sex offender notification procedures. Those efforts necessitate ethical considerations of what a stakeholder is not which includes that stakeholder theory does not necessarily mean equal treatment, it is not a comprehensive moral doctrine, nor is it equipped to provide specific objective functions in developing policies and practices (Hartman & DesJardins, 2008, p. 86).

Systemic Review of Sex Offender Management Strategies

An ongoing issue with regards to sex offenders is whether to prosecute as a criminal matter or treat as a civil matter. Civil commitment programs parallel to medical explanations for criminal behavior which is an ongoing debate among scholars and experts. Recent research considers the use of civil commitment as an extension of criminal commitment rather than separating the two as separate entities (Miller, 2010). Civil commitments are characteristically expensive and prolonged for high-risk sex offenders. Recidivism rates for those individuals are based on clinical and actuarial (mechanical, formal) methods that are based on the loose term of "likelihood." There is a great need to bridge the gap between the identified population and predictive accuracy practices (Vrieze & Grove, 2007). Specialized populations of sex offenders, i.e. developmentally disabled is beyond the scope of this case study other than brief inclusions of information.

Unlike any other category of crime, the sex offender registry and sex offender notification systems suggest that recidivism can be lowered by avoiding convicted offenders and by viewing people suspiciously. That practice raises a new theoretical question, "Have we reduced crime or displaced criminals?" With the majority of sexual crime being committed by family members and/or acquaintances, the real issue may be a reduction in reporting rather than a reduction in crime or a lowered recidivism (Prescott & Rockoff, 2011). Risk appraisal of sexual recidivism has traditionally been researched from a linear additive model; however, that approach negates the individuality characteristics of offenders. Nonlinear dynamics are examined in decision tree methods and time series forecasting that allow for intercorrelation of variables and subgroups that move away from a homogenous image of sex offenders (Bani-Yaghoub, Fedoroff, Curry, & Amundsen, 2010).

The Sex Offender Treatment Intervention and Progress Scale (SOTIPS) is an aid for clinicians, correctional caseworkers, and probation and parole officers utilizing a scale of sixteen dynamic risk factors and will score relative needs of treatment and supervision (McGrath, Cumming, & Lasher, 2012.) STATIC-99R is a coding form that includes age at release, relationships, conviction history and sentences, and detail about the victim's gender or familiarity to the offender (Retrieved from Static-99 Website). The Indiana Risk Assessment

System (IRAS) is a compilation of testing tools used specifically by IDOC and the (the facility). It was developed by the University of Cincinnati and is a proven tool for the Ohio Department of Corrections (Indiana Risk Assessment System, 2011).

Economic Considerations

Broken down to its simplest financial expense, incarceration costs for inmate population costs $54.28 per diem for each offender with an average total budget of $1,371,601.32 per day to house the offender population in IDOC. Indiana's total budget for 2010-2011 was $691.6 million (The Impact of Education and Employment on Recidivism, 2012). The economics of the sex offender services systems from a business standpoint is irrational at best. With current numbers that include rates of crime, numbers incarcerated, and persons on parole, there is good cause to explore private versus public production of services required. Scrutinizing the business model for supplying the demand of services expected from the public is more than justified (McEachern, 2012, p. 368).

(the corporation) provides government-outsourced services in the field of corrections, detention, and re-entry, including two Indiana facilities. The (the facility) is a 3,196-bed facility and the Plainfield S.T.O.P. location is a 1,066-bed facility making (the facility) location one of the largest privatized facility sites in the U.S. ((the corporation) Annual Corporate Report, 2011). In total, the U.S. presently has 739,853 registered sex offenders (RSOs) nationwide. Only 2 – 4% of that number includes those whose whereabouts are uncertain which invites a discussion of the effective use of services to satisfy a limited number of stakeholders (Ackerman, Levenson, & Harris, 2012). (the corporation) can achieve economies of scope within its current business model as there are ". . . significant commonalities between one or more of the value chain functions . . . that result in increased profitability (Hill & Jones, p. 317)."

Personal Interviews

Jennifer French, (the facility), Assistant Superintendent of Reentry & Programs (personal interview on October 29, 2012).

"The common denominator in the realm of the judicial system, corrections, and parole is the offender. In the past, sex offenders have been subject to a needs-based approach for services while incarcerated."

Ms. French pointed out that a previous approach to corrections is the differentiation between mental health issues and sex offender status which establishes program participation and is determined by an analysis of risks. When a person enters the Reception Diagnostic Center (hereafter referred to as RDC), a Prison Intake Tool is administered which identifies that person's risk areas.

"Currently, we are moving to a risk assessment which assists with a case plan based on five domains of risk. The three phases of SOMMS is considered a wraparound service; however, Indiana has recently included a new tool called Indiana Risk Assessment System that was born out of a project between IDOC and the University of Cincinnati."

"It would be interesting to compare and contrast recidivism rates between those on probation and those on parole, although no particular agency tracks that information. It would also be beneficial to categorize technicalities and look at percentages of who has returned to prison for what particular violation."

"When I was new to corrections, violating someone on a technicality seemed trivial until someone with greater experience told me, 'If a person cannot comply with small rules, they will not be able to transition to the larger rules of society.'"

"The system lacks interagency communication and needs to strengthen itself with evidence-based practices. There is no clear protocol for return inmates."

"There is a need for more meaningful statistics, which poses a question, 'Is there an acceptable percentage for recidivism?'"

"To some degree, we can suggest that violations on technical points suggest that a person cannot obey small rules; therefore, they will not succeed in transitioning to the larger rules of society."

When asked for general observations about the sex offender registry and parole stipulations as they relate to recidivism, Ms. French shared that there is stratification – staggered reasons why violations occur. Violators come back but there is minimal interagency communication. Presently there are no evidence-based practices attached to specific failures. Inaccuracies are problematic as there are unanswered questions, such as "Why did they do what they did?" The (the facility) has a unique approach to case management as the question is asked, "What is detrimental for the individual?" When those areas are identified, the case management plan focuses on those areas, i.e. a drug addict that cannot read needs both literacy and substance abuse group. The standard at (the facility) is a 6th- to 8th-grade reading level to participate in substance abuse class.

"That is not a statewide prerequisite but an evidence-based approach that (the facility) has adopted. Our case managers are the gateway to programs."

Thomas Lunay, House RX of Indiana, President / Founder, (telephone interview on October 29, 2012).

"After serving 25 years in IDOC as a sex offender and one year on parole and now working with IDOC and community partners to alleviate the housing crisis for reentry, I have a unique lens from which to view the registry, parole and recidivism."

"My conjecture is that parole is more like a reduced security level and serves no real function in transitioning from prison to community. On the one hand, parole boards have too much autonomy, yet part of their function is to keep people from scamming the system. The parole agent has just so much latitude in their decision-making and then they have to go to their regional director who, in turn, goes to the parole board which makes the whole system top heavy with bureaucracy."

"Parole agents and parolees both operate in fear. The agents fear that one of their cases might make the evening news which will cause the public to point their finger at the agent for failing the system by using the very processes that they are obligated to perform. The parolee feels like they are walking through a booby-trapped field that is inevitably going to end with their failure. Fear becomes the driving factor more than successful reentry to the community."

Victoria Fafata, Indiana Parole District #9, Supervisor (personal interview on November 7, 2012).

"As Parole Supervisor over eleven Indiana counties with a total count of 1,156 parolees, our agents have an average caseload of 101.5 offenders. Of that total, 140 are sex offenders." Ms. Fafata has been in corrections/parole since 1980. With her many years of experience, the question was asked, "How many of the 140 sex offenders does your experience say will make it successfully without a return to incarceration?" Ms. Fafata, "Less than half." Asked about her insights concerning the sex offender registry and parole stipulations, Ms. Fafata shared that, "The more you monitor, the more likely you are to "catch"? In that regard, the insight suggested that the intensity of supervision has the potential to be counterproductive. Ms. Fafata shared the insight that sex offenders are very good at hiding and/or getting away from what they do. She noted a case where an offender had been out for several years and was seemingly successful with aftercare and compliance only to discover that he was acting out in the same behaviors. Her observation concluded that sometimes all we teach is techniques to master the systems rather than to overcome behavior. Her perception is that the "lumping together" of sex offenders is the biggest problem. Early studies addressed crossover which led to the lumping together. She shared that studies in the 1990's concluded that if the first victim choice was not available to an offender that the perpetrator would move to a second victim choice which is partially the logic behind having offenders with crimes against adults subject to the same stipulations as those with crimes against minors/children.

Ms. Fafata was asked about her insights to the overall system. She shared that many times, we have had knee-jerk reactions, yet it is essential to remember that we cannot do the absolute. Many times, well-intended strategies have only driven sex offenders further underground. In her opinion, public education is critical to overcoming sexual offenses. "It is important that someone who has experienced questionable behavior go to someone. The conversation can confirm what did or did not happen. It is just as important for adults as it is for children to have someone to talk to about what happened." She shared valuable insights about parole agents walking a fine line between protection and service. Each agent wears multiple hats, and being proactive comes from knowing when to switch from social worker to law enforcement. Agents walk the line every day with their decision making.

Further in our conversation, a question was posed about sexually violent predators (SVPs). Ms. Fafata clarified that there is a difference between sexually violent predators and violent offenders. There are sexual predators who are not necessarily violent and violent offenders who are not necessarily going to commit sexual acts. While SVPs live under the 1,000 ft. rule for their residence, a murderer can be released from prison and have no residency restrictions. There is a need to separate out the question, "Who do you need to protect?" Ms. Fafata confirmed that it is extremely important for offenders to know while they are still incarcerated, that parole is not freedom. Rather, it is an extension of incarceration. There is still a need for improving the period of adjustment between incarceration in a facility and living on parole.

Penny Marcum, Henry County Sheriff's Department, Secretary (interview by phone on November 8, 2012).

"The State of Indiana has a fairly new Offender Watch system. When someone is released from DOC, the Watch notifies the person by whatever DOC has entered into the systems that they have to register. The system then triggers a message to the Sheriff's Department."

"The County watches for the person to come in by no more than seven days. Predators have only three days. If the time passes, a notification goes to Sheriff Butch Baker or Major Jay Davis to remind the person to come and register."

Ms. Marcum stated that typically a warrant is not immediately issued as the Sheriff's Department strives to investigate first as to what the delay might be about. In the case of an unregistered predator, there is a possibility for a warrant to be immediately issued. The second way that a person has to notify is if they are not incarcerated but placed on probation, and it is included in their terms of probation.

"The Sheriff knows who is liable for the 1,000 ft. rule, particularly with offenders against children and those with victims under the age of 12 years and predators. Each case is different."

When asked what her insights are about the registry, Ms. Marcum stated, "I don't think it is going to stop anyone from reoffending, but it helps public awareness. The public can take a look at where these persons are living and can at least be aware of those that are known."

The question about Ms. Marcum's experience with the registry brought his response, "I have worked with this since 2000. When I first started, it was a file folder with a few papers in it, but as time went by the State expanded the laws and requirements. Since 2002-2003, there has been a lot more work done on the system. Major Jay Davis works closely with the registry."

"Every offender is assigned to a specific deputy that checks on them at least four times a year which is more than is required. Henry County presently has 77 on the registry. Sixty-eight of those are active which means the rest are reincarcerated."

When asked about training, Ms. Marcum said, "Major Davis and I go to annual training to receive updates to programs and to learn about any changes in the law. Henry County does more than the State of Indiana requires and is diligent in their work with the registry."

Supposition from the Literary Review

With industry buzzwords like multidisciplinary treatment, collaboration, recidivism, stakeholders, and public health, it is easy to get lost in the conglomeration of research, public perception, legislation, and media until the waters are muddied beyond the average person's ability to sort it all out. What is true? What is not? Have sexual offenses become the new epidemic in the United States? Has sexual crime taken on Loch Ness monster proportions in the minds of the public, or is this a real phenomenon that must be given the highest priority for intervention and prevention? Is stranger danger a myth or fact? Researchers give disturbing statistics about 70% of all victims being under the age of 18 and half of that number being under the age of 12.

High profile sexual crimes have led to Megan's Law, The Jacob Wetterling Crimes Against Children Act, and the Adam Walsh Act, yet research holds a question begging to be answered, "Have these laws been effective in reducing new crimes and/or reducing recidivism?" The sex offender registry and sex offender notification laws attempt to offer peace of mind that this crisis is being brought under control, yet we have to know that almost all sexual victims have been victimized by someone they know – either a relative or acquaintance. How do we warn our children of someone who is living in the same house or within the family or a family acquaintance? We have taught them well to not take candy from a stranger, but our society has not been effective in dealing with familiarity between offender and victim.

The public only knows that the State of Indiana has a recidivism rate of almost 40% with a rate of nearly 70% for sex offenders, but do they know that those numbers are comprised largely of technical violations and not new crimes? Only 1.05% is the rate of return for new sexual crimes, yet the media continues to paint nightmarish pictures in the minds of the general public who, in turn, expect legislators to enact laws to bring this calamity to an end. The prison and jail population explosion and the massive increase in correctional expenditures have brought the United States to the forefront of industrialized nations who incarcerate its citizens with an increasingly insurmountable price tag attached. To examine the details of this puzzle, we need evidence-based practices, change management, strategic planning, and development of a shared diagnosis. This case study in its completed form will steer us toward critical thinking that operates from the rational mind, sociocentric thinking, conceptual analysis, and a reframing of ideologies that will meet the needs of the public to feel safe and to serve more effectively with reentry for offenders released to parole.

The new agenda to define sexual victimization as a public health crisis is focused on a victim-centered approach. The chief activity of anything defined as a public health issue is the inclusion of educating the stakeholders. With the opportunity to shed new light on the systemic areas that are weakened, the complete case study being submitted will offer solutions that include privatization, restructuring the organizational culture and structure of parole, and determining a more thorough means of transitioning from prison to reentry. With several thousand individuals on parole in the State of Indiana, it is essential to implement Lewin's field theory in social science and achieving mutual engagement. Including static and dynamic factors in assessments will close gaps for service providers to develop supportive and directive programming.

Research concerning accountable prisons and therapeutic prisons raises the bar for correctional facilities to pioneer a new course for competitive advantage and core capabilities. Exploring options with electronic monitoring technology, deepening collaboration with local police departments, and the inclusion of faith-based organizations will assist in refreshing policies and procedures for implementation. Rudes' research utilizes California's New Parole Model as a pattern for best practices and offers a new standard for prisons to shift their role from caretaker to service provider. Ethical consideration of public policy does not mean that the legislation is producing moral documents. Determinations have to be made as to whether to prosecute criminally or charge with civil treatment. Ultimately, we are left with the question, "Have we reduced crime or displaced criminals?"

While there is a fair amount of research available on the topics of the sex offender registry, parole stipulations for sex offenders, and recidivism, it is only 21 years in development and yet has areas that are lacking. Some of the questions that remain include, "Do individuals on probation have a lower recidivism than those on parole?" If the answer is affirmative, the obvious next question is, "Why?" For those who are violated on technicalities, the question exists, "What is the breakdown of the violations and why does one occur more than another?" A question posed in the interview with Jennifer French, "Is there an acceptable recidivism rate for any state, and if so, how would that be determined?" The information presented in the bibliography represents only a small sampling of available research and like any thorough consideration, in the end there is a whole new set of questions raised. The inquiry that this case study brings centers on whether current parole stipulations for sex offenders bring unavoidable technical violations that are actually falsely inflating the recidivism rates? Are the sex offender registry requirements an effective means of controlling sexual offenders from committing a new offense?

The major management issues that will be faced in the case study include implementation of policies and procedures and the selection of sex offender management treatment options. Addressing public perception without increasing fear and anxiety for the victims, their families, and communities will be a significant factor. The case study for this project will address details that other research projects have overlooked and will offer suggestions that are not present in the articles reviewed. A snapshot view of returns to incarceration based on technical violations for 2012 is included to illustrate a trend that has previously been undocumented by IDOC. The project will consider privatization, business ventures, further use of technology, more detail in the stratification of the parole caseload, and other organizational restructuring.

Analysis of the Issues

The legal address of sexual offenses is not new to this nation. The abduction of Jacob Wetterling in 1989, and the ensuing search for him set precedence in collecting leads and information into a database. That database became the foundation for legislation that was enacted in 1994 known as the Jacob Wetterling Crimes Against Children and Sexually Violent Offender Registration Act. The rape and murder of 7-year old Megan Kanka by a neighbor that was a known pedophile inspired legislation that broadened the registry to include notification of residency. On the 25th anniversary of his abduction and murder, Congress passed the Adam Walsh Child Protection and Safety Act in 2006. With legislation in place, it seems that we are headed the right direction for public safety, yet the questions posed earlier still begs to be asked, "Is there a societal benefit in rethinking the sex offender registry from the intent of its original function as it applies to parole stipulations for released sex offenders?" The second question is, "Are recidivism rates, IDOC specifically, falsely inflated due to parole technical violations by sex offenders?" Both questions are posed with positive intentions toward furthering the agenda of public safety, reduction in sexual crimes, and successful community reentry by those convicted of sexual crimes. For this case study, we examine the issues through the Indiana Department of Corrections and Parole Supervision Division as well as (the corporation) as a possible partner to alternative strategies as well as various management principles and theories presented throughout the Masters in Management Program with Indiana Wesleyan University.

"In the United States, sex offender registration is conducted at the local level and the federal government does not have a system for registering sex offenders (Sex Offender Registration and Notification in the United States, p. 1)." Although Congress has set minimum standards for the states and attached eligibility for certain grants to those standards, the actual work with the registry remains with law enforcement at the local level. "Effective January 1, 2003, Zachary's Law required sheriff's departments to jointly establish the Indiana Sex and Violent Offender Registry . . . to inform the general public about the identity, location, and appearance of sex and violent offenders who live, work, or study in Indiana (Sex & Violent Offender Registry, 2012)." Residential restrictions are severe such that an individual who may have been a longstanding homeowner prior to a conviction may not return to that housing if its location violates restrictions. Convicted sex offenders are not eligible for any federally subsidized housing. Homeless or transient sex offenders are an ongoing issue in regards to compliance with residency stipulations. A particular housing challenge is the location for releases that are facilitated under a program called DOC Assist whereby IDOC pays for a motel for the initial two weeks of release. The location of most DOC-assist housing is noted by high-crime, known drug trade/use areas of a city which often results in parolees functioning under pressures similar to a high-wire act with no safety net. Charting the correlation between sexual crimes and substance abuse is yet another area that demands further study and subsequent policies and practices that support rather than threaten successful reentry.

An ongoing challenge that exists in the application of the registry and notification laws is found in the many lawsuits filed by those directly impacted – the offenders. *Jensen v. State*, 905 N.E.2d 384, 396-98, (Ind. 2009) resulted in a 4-1 ruling by the Indiana Supreme Court that, ". . . classifying a man a sexually violent predator . . . doesn't violate Indiana's prohibition of ex post facto laws or the doctrine of separation of powers (Nelson, 2011)." In the case of *Patrick Fields v. Edwin G. Buss*, the plaintiff alleged that participation in the SOMMS program violated his constitutional rights regarding the Fifth Amendment, although the U.S. District Court Southern District of Indiana ultimately ruled that the self-incrimination clause applies only to evidence used during a criminal case and is not applicable to the program stipulations of self-disclosure (*Patrick Fields v. Edwin G. Buss,* 1:09-cv-00603-TWP-DML, 2011). *Michael Greer and John Maggi v. Edwin Buss, et al.* is a lawsuit filed against IDOC requiring 10-year registration periods from the perspective that the sex offender registry is a punitive action, particularly in the case of additional registration years added for new crimes beyond the initial 10-year period (Hoskins, 2010).

As uncomfortable as it may be for many readers, there is no question that multiple studies and research have come to the same conclusion regarding the sex offender registry. It has not proven to be the tool the public hoped for when they advocated for legislation. One of the strongest identified deficiencies in the registry and notification methodology is the treatment of sex offenders as a homogenous group. Referring back to the interview with Victoria Fafata, Supervisor of Parole District #9, we recount the research trend that nearly twenty years ago suggested a crossover of sexual offenses and a primary vs. secondary victim choice by offenders. Both of those ideas have since been repeatedly disproven, yet that school of thought remains the foundation for current practices. That, in part, speaks to our first analysis question concerning the validity of the registry from its original intent. Other than treatment consideration for special populations of offenders, the average conviction for sexual offense will lead to incarceration followed by parole and/or probation and community monitoring. For this case study, only parole is included with no discussions of probation.

Prison, Parole, and Regulating

Rapid change is the new norm in our society. The relationship between time and change is exponential in the United States. The paradigm shift is from bureaucracy to infocracy, yet the corrections industry is still rooted in the former model. "The new information-based paradigm requires new thinking values, systems, skills, as well as new kinds of leadership (Clawson, p. 58)." A documented truth is that prisons have largely failed as an influence in reducing recidivism, yet prisons remain at the core of crime-control efforts, particularly via the "get tough on crime" campaigns. A backfire phenomenon known in the medical world is called the "iatrogenic effect" which means the treatment increases patient harm. Many would suggest that has been the fate of prisons in relation to recidivism. "The Accountable Prison" by Cullen, Johnson, and Eck released in March 2012 shares the following recommendations:

- Lessons from police practitioners in moving from failure to success;

- Using what we know about effective rehabilitation;

- Use of three key principles – risk principle, need principle, and responsivity principle;

- Use of carrots (mostly) and sticks (not often) for incentive accountability.

The conclusion is that we choose a different future. Prison practices in the U.S. have mostly placed the burden of crime control on the prison outcomes. With a $52 billion annual price tag, the glaring truth is that the only crime control variable that is relative is to those who are serving their sentence. The system has controlled but not corrected.

A new light being offered to this topic is that of a therapeutic prison. In this model, the prison and not the offender is analyzed with a Correctional Program Inventory Assessment (hereafter referred to as CPIA). The earliest "reformatories" were based on Christian principles of transforming, ". . . the criminally wayward into citizens with strong moral fiber (Smith & Schweitzer, p. 7)." That methodology has long been cast aside through various Constitutional challenges and lawsuits that now have practicing religions inclusive of Rastafarianism, Buddhism, Paganism, Satanism, Islam, and several other faith practices beyond Christianity. For a therapeutic prison, the principle goal is to craft a productive experience that will translate to appropriate socialization after reentry. The CPAI has two primary areas – capacity and content that have a total of eight domains under the two headings.

Electronic monitoring technology has become more common within the past several years. IDOC enacted this policy in early 2012 with the use of a limited number of GPS tracking devices placed on individuals released to parole. The use of technology is part of the Adam Walsh Child Protection and Safety Act (2006). "The purposes of current devices are to allow an alternative to incarceration, to increase compliance, and to assist offenders with reintegrating into society (International Association of Chiefs of Police, p. 3)." In addition to the GPS tracking devices, other functions of monitoring technology include polygraphs, random calling and voice verification, remote alcohol monitoring, sleep pattern analysis, and motion detecting analysis. These options open the door for more collaboration between local law enforcement and parole supervisors and can improve data accuracy for information posted on public sex offender registries. IDOC's system is presently too new to have accumulated data to prove or disprove its usefulness. An attached inquiry is to research data concerning how many of those returning on technical violations were released under GPS monitoring. That information is presently not available through IDOC or Parole.

Parole serves a three-fold function, ". . . as an extension of the formal sentence, a form of early release, and a primary method of reducing prison overcrowding (Rudes, p. 1)." In order to rethink parole, the crucial hurdle of mobilizing support for change is nearly a brick wall as it is perceived to be softening on crime. A foundational intention of this case study is to inspire, if not provoke, the realization that there is a need for change. Change implementation theories, strategic renewal, and recognizing organizational capabilities construct a three-fold cord that will fortify efforts toward the sex offender registry and those accountable for enforcing its stipulations. ". . . a trigger event – a shift in the environment that precipitates a need for altered strategies and new patterns . . . (Spector, p. 18)" is what inspired the registry's existence, and now it is time to examine current trigger events and adjust accordingly. IDOC and its Parole Division are both completely equipped with staff that is more than capable of functioning with excellence in their field. With our later consideration of (the corporation) and its international reputation for superior services, the organizational challenges can be met.

For this level organizational change, we recommend the use of framing analyses, which are interactive procedures used to, ". . . locate, perceive, identify, and label people and events . . . assist individuals with understanding social contexts and making decisions within them (Rude, p. 3)." While parole agents are used to reincarcerating problem individuals, frame analyses redirects that decision making to keeping offenders in the community. The value of this is that parole middle managers, in particular, are given authority for street-level implementation plans. While the ideal caseload of 30 offenders is a rarity, parole agents are constantly challenged with maintaining quality of supervision. For parole officers, the presence of extralegal factors overlapping to the legal factors can spark a debate concerning the 14th Amendment's call for due process of law. Because the populations of prison and parole interchange frequently, it is worthwhile to examine their issues and resolutions with mutual consideration. With both venues, certain theories of change management and strategic management can assist in closing service gaps and relieving the seemingly unavoidable caveats. There is no question that whatever adjustments are willing to be made from an organizational perspective, a monumental challenge is prioritizing resources to bring the innovations to existence. Those resources include finance, building space, staff, instructors, supervisors, materials, time, and supplemental support systems. The economic picture for corrections is consistently, "do more with less" yet there are options to be explored and creative solutions to be considered.

"Parole authorities have been overlooked in regard to their potential establishing and sustaining meaningful change in correctional practice . . . serving as a systemic check on the administration of corrections (Paparozzi & Guy, p. 400)." With political appointments of an eclectic blend for state parole authorities, the result is a potpourri rather than a focused skill set that understands the dynamics of parole, its agents, and the offenders. Parole agents, like many other bureaucratic participants are overloaded, overworked, and underpaid which is a risk venture from a management perspective. They are subjected to a system known as venue sorting which is, ". . . the process by which cases are channeled between one or more organizational structures with distinct procedures and cultures . . . (Lin, Grattet, & Petersilia, p. 350)." Parole is particularly vulnerable to the three-fold standards of the criminal justice system: (1) the offender's perceived threat to public safety, (2) the offender's blameworthiness, and (3) the practical constraints of institutional bureaucracy (Linn, Grattet, & Petersilia, p. 352)." No other group of individuals on parole wears the label of social stigma like sex offenders. We do not have drug dealer registries (which perhaps does great overall harm by pure numbers and economics than any other group of felons). By nesting the venues (one within another) with more than one IDOC agency, it may be that there is more of a vested interest in parole revocation than would occur with parallel venues.

Law enforcement is the first direction the general public tends to look for any criminal issue. Yet, the practice continues that once an arrest is made local law enforcement's role is diminished as the individual moves on to other phases of the criminal justice system. "Collaborative partnerships for community policing and sex offender management are based on the recognition that public safety benefits can be maximized by respecting different perspectives, exchanging information, coordinating limited resources, and appreciating the complementary roles and responsibilities that exist within and across agencies and disciplines (Key Roles of Law Enforcement in Sex Offender Management, p. 2)." Applicable to this discussion is the following definition of local law enforcement, "Local law enforcement authority means the (1) chief of police of a consolidated city (i.e. the Indianapolis Metropolitan Police Department); or (2) the sheriff of a county that does not contain a consolidated city (i.e. the sheriff of all counties in Indiana except Marion County) (Sex and Violent Offender Registration Responsibility and Other Duties, 2012)."

Risk Assessment and Recidivism Prediction Instruments

The Indiana Risk Assessment System (hereafter referred to as IRAS) includes five instruments: (1) Pretrial (IRAS-PAT), (2) Community Supervision (IRAS-CST), (3) Screener (IRAS-CSST), (4) Prison Intake (IRAS-PIT, and (5) Reentry (IRAS-RT). For purposes of this case study, we will examine the IRAS-PIT and IRAS-RT in more detail. It is worthwhile to note that the Reentry tool is not administered until an individual has been incarcerated two years or more. A question that arises with waiting two years or more to administer a reentry tool is that it lacks a measurement of time extent effects from a person initially arriving into IDOC in order to determine if their reentry capabilities have deteriorated as a result of incarceration. A sampling of questions from both the IRAS-PIT and IRAS-RT are included in Appendix C. The professionals who administer these tools have participated in intensive training sessions and have completed examinations of their materials; therefore, it is not the intent of this case study to portray the writer's proficiency but to offer a summation of the assessment.

Most systems that address sexual offenses use an instrument called the STATIC-99 and, more recently, the STATIC-99R (revised). A copy of the STATIC-99R is included in Appendix D. This assessment is completed at the IDOC Reception and Diagnostic Center (RDC) in Plainfield, IN during an individual's initial 4-6 weeks of incarceration. Once convicted and sentenced, every offender spends time at this center to undergo a battery of educational, psychological, medical, and other testing in order to determine the best placement within IDOC. To comply with the Prison Rape Elimination Act (PREA), correctional facilities score individuals as a predator, victim, none, or a combination. This status is reviewed annually and is presented to a PREA Committee for final approval. These two assessments are briefly mentioned in this discussion as the system has a duty to be aware of sexual predators within a corrections facility and protect other offenders as much as it has an obligation to the general public.

Also briefly included is the issue of individuals who commit sexual crimes and are determined to be developmentally disabled or have other mental health diagnoses. An additional concern with sex-offender specific studies is that of civil commitments that are enforced beyond serving prison sentences. "No matter how hard is recidivism to detect, the passage of sexually violent person (SVP) commitment laws . . . mandates that recidivism predictions about individuals be made (Vrieze & Grove, p. 263)." Engaging in a detailed discussion of mental abnormalities or personality disorders relative to sexual offenses is beyond the scope of this case study; however, it is included as part of addressing apprehensions by the general public concerning individuals using an "insanity plea" to avoid imprisonment. Many see, ". . . treatment is a gateway to release . . . yet . . . few, if any, sexually violent predators are ever released from commitment (Miller, p. 2108).

Correctional professionals have traditionally used actuarial instruments for assessing an offender's risk of recidivism; however, that method is problematic in that it disregards time elements. For example, to predict recidivism, many states use clinical and actuarial methods while literature conjectures that one is as strong as the other; however few sex-offender specific studies have compared the two methods (Vrieze & Grove, 2007). With the many actuarially-based methods in use for sex offenders, it creates a void to not complete a comparison study specific to this group. Glenn D. Walters May 2010 report of predicting recidivism using psychological inventories of criminal thinking styles urges the use of, ". . . outside investigators to rule out the possibility of an allegiance effect (Walters, p. 218)" which supports the use of contractual agencies for conducting studies. The primary weakness of actuarial methods is that they are linear additive models that, by default, ignore overlap of factors and measure only static factors.

A study by Bani-Yaghoub et al examined two new streams of research – decision tree methods and time series forecasting – specific to sex offender risk for recidivism. Using acute, static, and dynamic variables to construct risk values along with age brackets and time intervals the team was able to identify patterns of fluctuation. As stated early in this case study, ". . . any prediction of violent or sexual re-offense will always carry some degree of error (Bani-Yaghoub et al, p. 364)." The newer methods demonstrated marked improvement in accuracy but leave an invitation open to further integrate the methods and incorporate nonlinear time series techniques. A three-wave prospective study concerning criminal recidivism centers on static and dynamic risk factors. ". . . static risk factors such as criminal history are considered constant and unchanging, thus not amenable to treatment . . . dynamic risk factors, such as substance abuse and criminal attitudes can change, and, consequently are amenable to treatment (Brown, St. Amand, & Zamble, p. 25)."

The use of three or more waves in a study strengthens the possibility of detecting changes in dynamic variables, thus increasing predictive accuracy. One strong predictor of recidivism is the combination of two static factors – SIR-R1 (Statistical Information on Recidivism Scale – Revision 1) and prison misconduct. A critical conclusion from this study, ". . . would indicate that variables currently classified as 'triggers' should be re-classified perhaps as 'response mechanisms' (Brown, St. Amand, & Zamble, p. 42)" which, in turn, confirms the goal of community supervision to stabilize the offender's lifestyle. Recommendations by the researchers included incorporating more self-reporting to balance the official information and to consider phases of release.

Strategies, Policies, and Practices

The recent shift toward evidence-based practices by criminal justice and correctional policymakers is expected to increase public safety by maximizing resources. The unfortunate downside to this trend is that the same movement has not yet taken hold in the development of sex-offender specific policies by legislators. The variety of typologies and variations between states has created a patchwork of public policy. Poor cross-jurisdictional coordination creates confusion not only for those obligated to the registry but to law enforcement and parole agents. For example, in the State of Indiana, ". . . laws mandate that convicted offenders live at least 305 m (1,000 ft.) from a school, public park, or youth program center; however, the State of Illinois only requires that offenders live at least 152 m (500 ft.) away from a school (Grubesic & Murray, p. 671)." Spatial saturation laws are designed to restrict a clustering of sex offenders in any one (the corporation)graphical area. "Ironically, in a report issued by the Colorado Department of

Public Safety, it was found that high-risk sex offenders living in 'shared living arrangements' were less likely to recidivate (Grubesic & Murray, p. 673)." Although there are multiple pages of uniform requirements concerning the registry, a definite issue attached to the sex offender registry along with enforcement and supervision is the multiplicity of guidelines across the range of local, county, and/or state jurisdictions.

It is beyond the scope of this case study to examine in detail the distinctions between the registry and notification requirements concerning recidivism. One study neatly packages the expectations of the registry with this statement, "The public can, in theory, reduce sex offender recidivism by avoiding convicted offenders and reporting suspicious behavior (Prescott, p. 4)." An issue question that arises from that level of thinking is to inquire whether the registry reduces crime or displaces it. There remains a great need to study sexual offenses and the offenders in categories, i.e. rape, child molestation, prostitution, pornography, etc. The mixed results that are consistently portrayed through most research do not promote the ability to identify inclusive strategies. Perhaps the most stunning statistic offered is this, "Sex offenses represent under 1% of all arrests (CSOM Fact Sheet: What you need to know about sex offenders, 2012)." That singular statement raises a plethora of questions, such as, "Why has the American public put such an intense focus on sexual crimes versus other crimes that cause social harm, i.e. drug trafficking and use?"

Conclusion

The first step necessary to offer any substantial conclusions is to determine a diagnosis. "Diagnosis is meant to create learning about the real, current, and unique dynamics impacting the organization's performance . . . diagnosis is about learning what needs to be changed and why (Spector, p. 59)." More importantly, it is crucial that all those involved change in the same direction; therefore, a coordinated change is the hub of this turning wheel. Coordinated change can only occur when there is mutual engagement of all stakeholders. Utilizing the principles of Lewin's three stages of change implementation – unfreezing, moving, and refreezing - can aid policymakers, practitioners, and public perception in transitioning to more operative approaches to the questions posed in this case study. "All forms of learning and change start with some form of dissatisfaction or frustration . . . (Spector, p. 29)." For actual unfreezing, the disconcerting information has to connect to something the stakeholders care about, which in this case is public safety and successful reentry. Upon closer consideration, this study is compelled to ponder whether the public has now or has ever had a burden for reentry or has the public restricted its concerns to its own safety. Can one exist without the other? That question has yet to be addressed. Without actualizing results that positively impact victims and offenders, we are at-risk for quickly becoming a caste society. Much of the unfreezing and preparation for change implementation will come from educating the public to an uncomfortable truth – the sex offender registry has not accomplished its hoped-for goals and objectives neither has incarcerating offenders on technical violations promoted or preserved community reentry.

Among the many strategies of political influence, ". . . evidence indicates that rational persuasion, inspirational appeals, and consultation tend to be the most effective (Robbins & Judge, p. 184)." In particular, rational persuasion is proven to be useful with all three directions of influence – upward, downward, and lateral. Rational persuasion is defined as, "Presenting logical arguments and factual evidence to demonstrate that a request is reasonable (Robbins & Judge, p. 184)." In responding to the two questions to be answered by this case study, it is inevitable that rational persuasion must be fused into any conclusions that are proposed. The foundation of any other offerings to this topic is laid with a sweeping two-tiered campaign of public education. One tier has a focal point of correcting misnomers and reeducating the general public to a correctly drawn portrait of sexual offenses. The second tier is to match or surpass previous public education campaigns such as the HIV/AIDS Awareness. The second tier will necessitate sub-components for age-appropriate messages but can include the following platforms illustrated in Figure 6.

Figure 6 - *Suggested Public Awareness Venues*

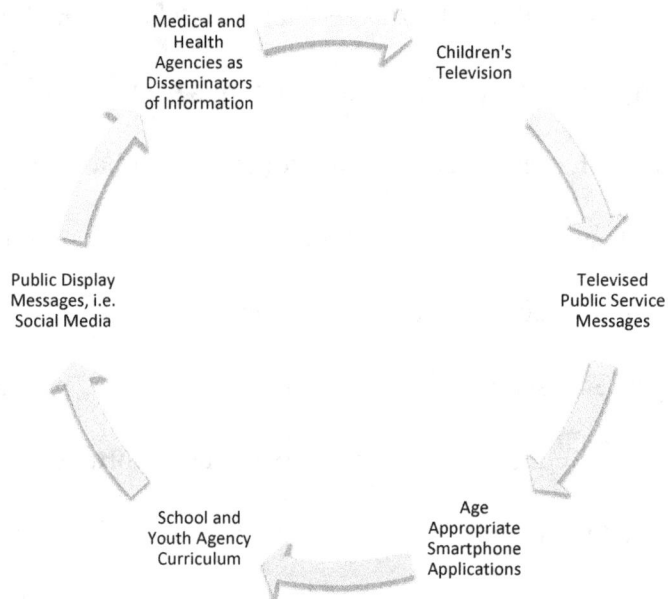

In total, the campaign is designed to break myths, correct misinformation, and strengthen the accuracy of perceptions by the public as the largest stakeholder group for this issue. With over 70 percent of victims under the age of 18 and half of that number under the age of 12, it is imperious that public education contains a campaign for educating children to awareness and reporting. The under-reporting of sexual crimes is a public concern matching or exceeding the reported crimes. "As such, the nature of the interactions between the investigating officer and the victim become a paramount consideration (Key Roles of Law Enforcement in Sex Offender Management, 2008)." Perhaps a campaign with a spokesperson for children would provide a positive image for increasing awareness and reporting. Examples of other successful campaigns include Smokey the Bear and McGruff the Dog. The adult voice of the American public must intercede for our children and must cultivate a proactive environment.

Despite multiple studies and conclusions that long-term recidivism rates are lower for sex offenders than any other criminal group, particularly those who have received specialized treatment, there remains a need to address this group as a social priority. There are presently four assessments that may take place for a sex offender. Those include risk assessments, criminal justice assessments, clinical assessments, and ongoing, multidisciplinary assessments (Thigpen et al., 2011). It is the recommendation of this case study that those instruments be merged such that there is an evolutionary process toward a comprehensive assessment tool. The inclusionary assessment will be based on both static and dynamic variables and be viewed as a nonlinear model such that legal and extralegal factors may be considered. As long as our systems have a collaged approach to assessments, there will be no positive progress toward an evidence-based approach.

Beginning in 2005, Indiana's recidivism rate has dropped and is currently at 37.4%. The statistics concerning sex offenders are the most promising of all categories of offense with a 1.05% rate. That is one of the lowest in the United States (Indiana's Recidivism Rate Declines for Third Consecutive Year, 2009). No matter how small the recidivism rates are for new crime, there will remain a need to study those individuals and trends and develop strategies to thwart those actions. Because ethical decision making requires the involvement of one or more critical issues, it has been a goal of this case study to present a balanced perspective giving consideration to all stakeholders. In the discussion of the sex offender registry and the reduced recidivism rates that have sustained over a number of years, we must pose whether we are currently suffering from change blindness which means, ". . . decision makers fail to notice gradual changes over time (Hartman & DesJardins, p. 51)."

A previous citation noted that the ideal caseload for a parole agent is 30 parolees while Victoria Fafata confirmed that on average, the actual caseload is over 100 parolees. In light of the many assessments that are used to evaluate offenders and their risk potential to the community, it is timely to consider alternative reporting procedures that will increase thoroughness of reporting and ease the caseload activity for parole agents. Perhaps our decision makers would serve its public audience (stakeholders) more effectively by reassigning resources and attention to the most critical period of time for successful reentry. ". . . over one-third of the arrests for any new crimes took place within the first six months of release (Managing the Challenges of the Sex Offender Registry, p. 2)." The same research article concerning the challenges of the registry offers a tailored approach to reentry for sex offenders. Figure 7 demonstrates the 6-step approach to address the intense reentry needs of an offender's initial six-month after his/her out date.

Figure 7 - *Framework for Sex Offender Reentry Strategy*

Collaboration to Achieve an "In to Out" Approach
Manage Sex Offenders in Prison with an Eye Toward Release
Recognize the Value of Discretionary Release Decisionmaking
"Reach Out" During the Transition and Release Process
Ensure Victim-Centeredness in the Reentry Process
Adopt a Success-Oriented Approach in Post-Release Supervision

Seemingly a minor area of reentry but one that is deserving of its own study is the ability of parolees to continue in their spiritual faith beliefs. Many times over, it has been suggested to pastors to provide an "adults only" service. The goal is not to have an isolated sex offenders' service but to host a service that accommodates adult needs, i.e. senior citizens who may prefer a service with no children due to physical limitations, such as hearing impairment. Faith-based programming can be a major contributor to stabilizing the first six months (and beyond) for individuals released on parole through phone support lines, hosting groups, providing spiritual counseling, and more.

The cross-jurisdictional issues mentioned in another sub-section are also problematic for policies and procedures. The Indiana Court of Appeals has two recent cases that brought the Indiana Sex and Violent Offender Registry under legal scrutiny. In *David Schepers, et al., v. Commissioner, Indiana Department of Correction,* 11-3834, concerned correcting an erroneous listing while *Thomas Andrews v. State of Indiana,* 29A02-1112-MI-1166 argued that since Andrews committed his crime in Massachusetts that his move to Indiana excused him from registering in this state. In the first case, the issue was not actually with IDOC but with the Indiana Sheriff's Association who has the task of monitoring the registry (completed by each of the 92 Indiana counties). In the second case, Andrews was not subject to State prosecution but under the SORNA rules, he was subject to federal prosecution (Stafford, 2012). A possible inference from situations such as these is the need to centralize administration.

Sample and Kadleck's 2008 study explored the beliefs of policymakers in regards to sex offenders noted the following insights, (1) ". . . most legislators perceived sex offenders as a growing problem . . .; (2) . . . all respondents admitted to relying on the media to inform them of current trends . . . ; (3) legislators readily admit the need to pander to their constituents as a demonstration of their ability to respond to public concerns . . . (Grubesic & Murray, p. 680)." Some scholars propose that, ". . . sex offender policies can accomplish important symbolic objectives . . . can serve to inspire and reinforce social solidarity by uniting toward a commonly accepted goal (Ackerman et al, p. 2)." Public policy is a necessary element to the functions of our democratic society, yet we cannot become guilty of refusing the total responsibility. "Policy development at the national level has been driven largely by information provided by a limited circle of selected stakeholders, rather than by independently conducted empirical research (Ackerman et al, p. 8)." The Adam Walsh Act, in particular, provides federal standards for reporting and registration but has minimal influence on integrity, quality, or integration of data,

The initial efforts to obtain data that would categorize technical violation was met with, "No one has that kind of data." Technical violations refer to parole stipulations and do not include new crimes. The same response was given in discussion with Parole in regards to the cataloging of violations for further study. After review and categorizing of parole hearing conclusions (public information) that stipulated those for the (the facility), Figure 8 displays the results of first-time parole violators and the primary causes for a return to incarceration.

Figure 8 – *Code Total for Technical Violations / Parole Hearings 2012*

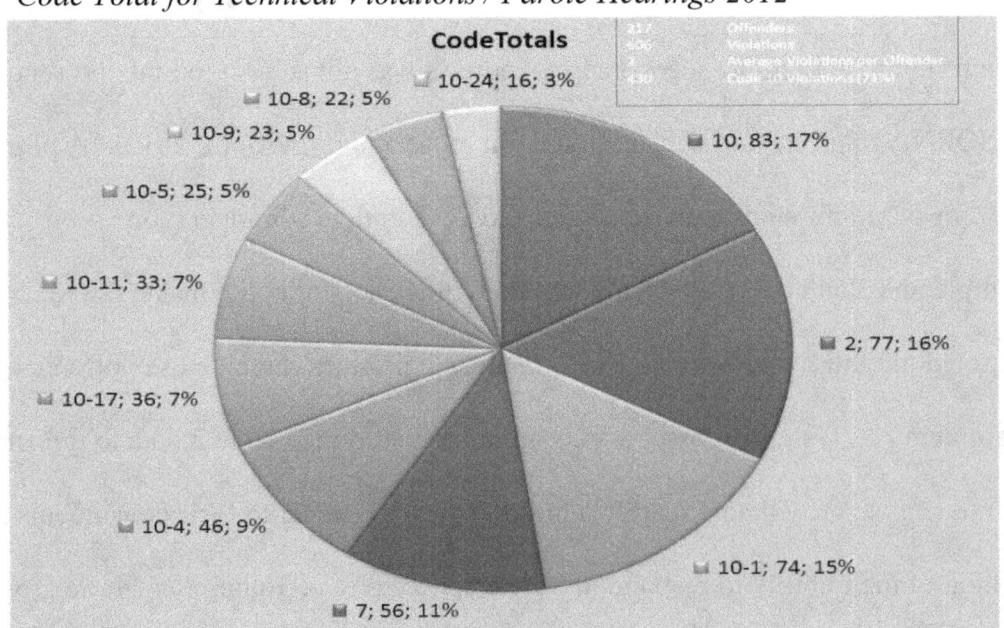

(color copy will be made available upon request to author by email)

It is imperative to note the frequency of number 10 violations, which come under the heading, "Communication and Special Instructions." It is judicious to consider an additional study to compare and contrast female offenders on parole with male offenders for the most recurrent technical violations. The high percentage of violations based on communication leads to consideration of multiple studies concerning men and communication which, in turn, directs us to consider whether a focal point of incarceration is to instruct in communication skills and techniques. More specifically, there may be a need to address communication skills when a person is under duress or experiencing variables that make daily living seem "out of control." There is also a need to study the combination of communication and special instruction violations in conjunction with other violations. For example, a 10-1 is communication and special instructions combined with enrollment, participation, and completion of an approved sex offender treatment program. It is possible to catalog the specific areas of failure to communicate and should be given further attention for research.

To offer conclusions about the questions posed for this case study, we need to divert slightly and incorporate some organizational principles. Whatever alterations need to be made to the sex offender registry and parole stipulations, they will have to be made through strategic view and direction. A proposed change in the thinking toward those agencies and organizations involved is to think in terms of a value chain. "A value chain is a stream of activities that add values to the inputs and make them desirable to others (Clawson, p. 70)." A broader view of this is to identify all of the separate activities and analyze the economics of each. Within each activity, we look at the collection of organizational skills and core capabilities. Then we look at strategic intent in order to have a future perspective on the industry. One of the key elements to strategic thinking is to understand the importance of timing. From this case study, it is reasonable to conclude that it is time to rethink the registry and to reconsider the pace of technical violations for those on parole, particularly with the primary solution remaining with further incarceration. As we weigh the many conclusions that point to the need for an independent party to participate in the process, we can readily turn our attention to (the corporation). As a for-profit, non-government entity, (the corporation) brings the privatization model to the table for consideration. This case study can only conclude that it would be in the best interests of all to implement a pilot program initially from the Indianapolis Parole District and initiate a contract with (the corporation) for its oversight.

(the corporation)'s organizational design is built on motivating its employees to perform at high levels which add credence to its capabilities to engage in a pilot program with IDOC's Parole Division. A particular player in this possibility is the (the facility) (privatized under (the corporation)) which has repeatedly proven its excellence with specialized housing units and programs. (the facility) presently has a housing unit specific to individuals with four or more years remaining on their sentence, a HOPE unit which housing individuals with developmental disabilities and/or mental health issues, a Sober Living Unit which houses graduates of the substance abuse program, a Short Term Offender Program (S.T.O.P.) Unit, Purposeful Living Units Serve (P.L.U.S.) and, most recently, a Veteran's Unit. Recidivism for those in P.L.U.S. has proven to be as much as 30 percent less than the state average. The curriculum for the P.L.U.S. unit might be evaluated as a core curriculum for all persons serving a current sentence; however, it is noteworthy that the P.L.U.S. unit is successful due to a combination of program components and not due solely to the instructional element. In addition, P.L.U.S. is an application program and not mandatory.

Currently, over 90 percent of the population at (the facility) is serving a sentence for a sexual crime. It is logistically sound to centralize that population for purposes of implementing treatment programs and efficiently concentrating resources. With its established adaptive culture, (the corporation) encourages its staff to explore innovative initiatives for services. "Functional structures group people on the basis of their common expertise and experience or because they use the same resources (Hill & Jones, p. 398)." With 60 percent of its business unit invested in corrections, (the corporation) is positioned to engage in initiatives with IDOC and Parole. The 2011 Annual Report includes a statement from (the corporation) Chairman of the Board that continuing trends toward specializing populations has allowed its U.S. Corrections and Detention Division to service unique groupings of offenders ((the corporation) Annual Report, p. 4). With its recent acquisition of BI Industries and expanded strategy titled *Continuum of Care*, (the corporation) adds to its value chain capabilities, particularly in the field of electronic monitoring. Achieving the status of a multi-billion dollar company in less than thirty years adds to the economic credibility of including (the corporation) as a partner to the task of regulating practices and monitoring those subject to the sex offender registry. The (the corporation) contract for the New Castle facility further opens the door to accurate cataloging and tracking of recidivism by examination of particular sexual crimes. Currently, that data is lost in the mix of generalized statements about recidivism.

There are wide possibilities for increased technological features to parole supervision that would alleviate the burden of officers and implement more thorough practices that could upgrade frequency and accuracy of reporting. While sex offenders may not access the internet with the exception of work searches, that option opens the door for increasing frequency of monitoring. With portable fingerprint scanners costing less than $100, parole could implement a program for low-risk offenders to check in with agents via a texting program on their cell phone or through collaboration with Work One Centers. Issuing cards similar to food stamp cards or public welfare benefit cards could also incorporate a means for offenders to 'swipe" their location, particularly if including the fingerprint device supported by monitoring software. Working with the automated JPay system already in place within IDOC offers an additional partner to this process. In this day and age of payment plans, technical violations for failure to pay fees could be all but eliminated by predetermining all required fees and setting up an account system with interest based on a payment plan. If that system could be tied to credit bureau reporting, it would add incentive to parolees to pay in order to build a positive credit score. There is a multitude of options available to strengthen reentry without compromising public safety or removing accountability from the offender. Resetting the goals from ostracizing and stigmatizing to strategizing is key to evolving into a win-win situation for society and the offenders.

The Center for Sex Offender Management offers multiple suggestions in its manual, *Twenty Strategies for Advancing Sex Offender Management in Your Jurisdiction*. For obvious reasons, this case study can only offer a macroscopic view of those strategies. Collaboration is the ongoing theme of an effective strategy. That can begin with something as small as setting common definitions and viewing date with a common lens. The definition of recidivism can change from one agency to the next and the interpretation of data is equally subjected to differences rather than similarities. To accomplish the victim-centered approach, IDOC and Parole might consider a third arm of liaison caseworkers. Those individuals would serve as a consultant to the two primary organizations involved with sex offenders as well as working to meet community needs. Reminding ourselves that the majority of victims are minors, there must be a link between parents or guardians and the systems involved. The other highlighted strategy from the manual is that of creating seamless exchange mechanisms versus the fragmentation that currently exists. That is mostly an Information Technology (IT) issue that like all other challenges posed can be resolved by the multitude of talented individuals already in place with the various agencies mentioned. If (the corporation) were to be engaged for a pilot program to privatize, they would be the perfect business partner for having the capacity to address this issue.

A principle strategy that has decades of proven research support it is the correlation between education and recidivism. Particularly when we look at the economics of recidivism (average recidivism at nearly 40 percent), the numbers speak loudly for themselves. Under former President Bill Clinton's administration, access to Pell Grants was removed for those incarcerated but as recently as this past year, other funding for private colleges continuing to work with prisons has been so drastically reduced as to render the concept impotent. Figure 9 portrays a compare and contrast model for considering costs of incarceration versus costs of education (based on annual tuition fees at Ball State University minus housing) along with education as a predictor of recidivism (Nally, Lockwood, & Ho, 2012).

Figure 9 - *Comparison of Employment, Education, and Recidivism*

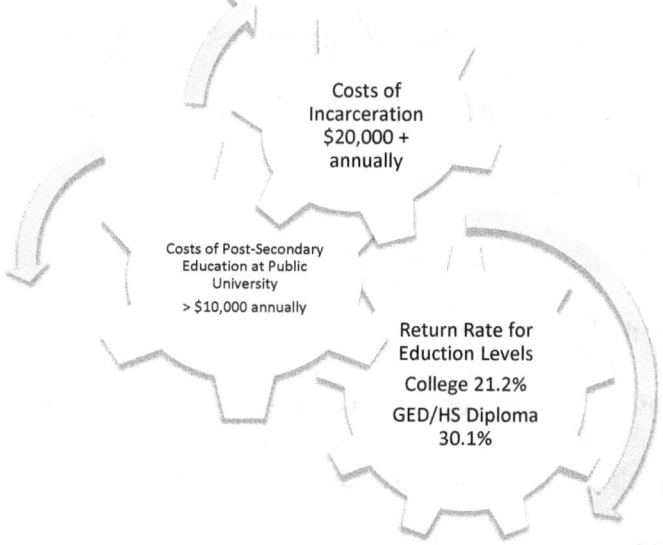

For all of the discussions that could be hosted concerning programs, policies, and so on, education for offenders has to be viewed through a different lens than in recent trends. "IDOC research shows that associate degrees have a much greater impact on inmate employment, once they are released, he said (Loughlin, 2011)." An inevitable conclusion is a necessity of reconsidering why legislation has removed a viable option for reducing recidivism by such drastic percentages. It is time to put education back on the table during the exploration of what keeps offenders out of prison. In fairness to that conversation, it also triggers a secondary study concerning educational levels of sex offenders versus those with other violent crimes. This writer is compelled to reiterate that there is a glaring gap in the data that is collected and/or how it is categorized.

Our first question, "Is there a societal benefit in rethinking the sex offender registry from the intent of its original function as it applies to parole stipulations for released sex offenders?" leads us to encourage the public, legislators, policymakers, and practitioners to agree that the answer is, "Yes, there are benefits for all stakeholders in reopening a discussion of the registry." Secondly, "Are recidivism rates, IDOC specifically, falsely inflated due to parole technical violations by sex offenders?" Again, we are compelled to respond in the affirmative. The second response begs a third question that was unasked in this case study, "Who benefits from inflated recidivism rates?" The answer might be that no one benefits, but to respond thoroughly, there is a need to examine funding sources and other secondary issues as well as the political influences on any department of corrections.

It seems that no matter which direction this case study takes, each question sparks more inquiry and causes us to see the chasm that exists across our questions and complete responses. Course constraints do not allow us to delve into many extended areas of discussion, such as comparison between U.S. culture and other nations in regards to reporting, law enforcement, and criminal justice responses to sex offenses, moral and/or spiritual influences and implications, possible correlations between non-traditional families and the victim-offender relationship (crossover groups mentioned in the initial portions of this paper), collateral consequences for both victim and offender families, friends, and communities and other sensitive areas of conversation that however uncomfortable most of us might be are nevertheless necessary to thoroughly examine the issue of sexual offenses in the United States. Above all, this case study absolutely has no part in blaming the victim, yet even the discussion of victims exposes other difficult and complex questions. Perhaps we are at fault as much with victims as we are with offenders by referring to them as a "one size fits all" or "lumping together" concept that cannot do justice to the many faces of victimization. Perhaps we are most guilty of a "stance of rational ignorance" which refers to public interest that, ". . . remains largely oblivious to most public choices (McEachern, p. 359)." Perhaps there is no ending to this case study other than to challenge and inspire ourselves through the words of World War II survivor Anne Frank, "How wonderful it is that nobody need wait a single moment before starting to improve the world." Even more specifically, Pastor Denise S. Millben of Muncie, IN said, "The difference between a burden and a concern is that when a person is concerned, they hope somebody will do something but when that person has a burden, they cannot stop until they do something." The final conclusion offered in this case study is that there is a need for a burden and not merely a concern about the sex offender registry and its implications to those on parole and its subsequent influence on recidivism rates.

References

Ackerman, A.R., Levenson, J.S., & Harris, A.J. (2012, March). How many sex offenders really live among us? Adjusted counts and population rates in five US states. *Journal of Crime and Justice*, 35(3), 464-474. DOI:10.1080/0735648X.2012.666407l.

Advancing Corrections. (2012). 2011 Annual Report: Indiana Department of Corrections. Retrieved from IDOC Website: http://www.in.gov/idoc/files/2011DOCAnnualReport.pdf

Agan, A.Y. (2011, February). Sex offender registries: Fear without function? *Journal of Law & Economics*, 54(1), 207-239. Retrieved from Ebscohost.

Bani-Yaghoub, M., Fedoroff, J.P., Curry, S., & Amundsen, D.E. (2010, October). A time series modeling approach in risk appraisal of violent and sexual recidivism. *Law & Human Behavior*, 34(5), 349-366. DOI: 10.1007/s10979-009-9183-y.

Bonnar-Kidd, K.K. (2010, March). Sexual offender laws and prevention of sexual violence or recidivism. *American Journal of Public Health*, 100(3), 412-419. Retrieved from Ebscohost.

Brown, S.L., St. Amand, M.D., & Zambie, E. (2009, February). The dynamic prediction of criminal recidivism: A three-wave prospective study. *Law & Human Behavior*, 33(1), 25-42. DOI: 10.1007/s10979-008-9139-7.

Clawson, J.G. (2009). The changing context of leadership. *Level Three Leadership: Getting Below the Surface,* 4th ed., 45-64. Upper Saddle River, NJ: Pearson Prentice Hall.

Clawson, J.G. (2009). The REB model. *Level Three Leadership: Getting Below the Surface,* 4th ed., 154-171. Upper Saddle River, NJ: Pearson Prentice Hall.

Clawson, J.G. (2009). Strategic frames. *Level Three Leadership: Getting Below the Surface,* 4th ed., 65-85. Upper Saddle River, NJ: Pearson Prentice Hall.

CSOM fact sheet: What you need to know about sex offenders. (2012). Retrieved from the

    Center for Sex Offender Management Website:

    http://www.csom.org/pubs/needtoknow_fs.pdf

Cullen, F.T., Johnson, C.L., & Eck, J.E. (2012, February). The accountable prison. *Journal of*

    Contemporary Criminal Justice, 26(4), 410-425. DOI:10.1177/1043986211432202.

Enhancing the Management of Adult and Juvenile Sex Offenders: A Handbook for Policymakers

    and Practitioners. (2007). Retrieved from the Center for Sex Offender Management

    Website: http://www.csom.org/pubs/CSOM_handbook.pdf

Fields v. Edwin G. Buss., (S.D. IN. 2011). (unpublished). Retrieved from Justice

    DocumentsWebsite: http://docs.justia.com/cases/federal/district-

    courts/indiana/insdce/1:2009cv00603/23382/70/0.pdf?1301679069

Greenleaf, R.K. (2008). *The Servant as Leader*, 9-61. Westfield, IN; The Greenleaf Center for

    Servant Leadership.

Grubesic, T. & Murray, A. (2009). Methods to support policy evaluation of sex offender laws.

    Papers in Regional Science, 89(3), 669-684. DOI:10.1111/j1435-5957.2009.00270.x.

Hartman, L.P. & DesJardins, J. (2008). Ethical decision making: Personal and professional

    contexts. *Business Ethics: Decision Making for Personal Integrity & Social*

    Responsibility, 2nd ed., 45-94. New York, NY: McGraw-Hill Irwin.

Hill, C.W. & Jones, G.R. (2010). Strategic leadership: Managing the strategy-making process for

    competitive advantage. *Strategic Management: An Integrated Approach*, 9th ed., 1-36.

    Australia: South-Western Cengage Learning.

Hill, C.W. & Jones, G.R. (2010). Implementing strategy in companies that compete in a single industry. *Strategic Management: An Integrated Approach*, 9th ed., 378-420. Australia: South-Western Cengage Learning.

Hoskins, M.W. (2010, January). COA rules on sex offender registration. *Indiana Lawyer*, 20(22), 5-6. Retrieved from Ebscohost.

Indiana Department of Corrections Adult Recidivism Rates. (2012). Retrieved from Indiana Department of Corrections Website:

http://www.in.gov/idoc/files/2011_Adult_Recidivism_Summary.pdf

Indiana Department of Corrections Recidivism Rates Decrease for 3rd Consecutive Year. (2009, March). Retrieved from Indiana Department of Corrections Website:

http://www.in.gov/idoc/files/IDOCRecidivism.pdf

Indiana parole. (2012). Retrieved from Government Registry Website:

http://www.governmentregistry.org/criminal_records/parole/state_parole/indiana_parole.

Indiana Risk Assessment System. (2011). Cincinnati, OH: University of Cincinnati Criminal Justice Research Center.

Kerbs, J.J., Jones, M., & Jolley, J.M. (2009, August). Discretionary decision making by probation and parole officers. *Journal of Contemporary Criminal Justice*, 25(4), 424-441. DOI:10.1177/1043986209344556.

Key Roles of Law Enforcement in Sex Offender Management. (2008, December). Retrieved from the Center for Sex Offender Management Website:

http://www.csom.org/pubs/law_enforcement_key_roles.pdf

Legislative trends in sex offender management. (2008, November). Retrieved from Center for Sex Offender Management Website: http://csom.org/pubs/legislative_trends.pdf

Letter to the shareholders. (Annual Report, 2011). Retrieved from (the corporation) Website:

http://www.(the corporation)group.com/documents/2011-report.pdf

Lin, J., Grattet, R., & Petersilia, J. (2012, October). Justice by other means: venue sorting in

parole revocation. *Law & Policy*, 34(4), 349-372. DOI:10.1111/j.1467-

9930.2012.00366.x.

Loughlin, S. (2011, May). Indiana Department of Correction changing inmate education.

Retrieved from Terre Haute Tribune Website:

http://www.indianaeconomicdigest.net/main.asp?SectionID=31&ArticleID=59972

Managing the challenges of sex offender reentry. (2007, February). Retrieved from the Center

for Sex Offender Management: http://www.csom.org/pubs/reentry_brief.pdf

Maxwell, J.C. (2007). The 360 degree leader. *The Maxwell Leadership Bible*, 2nd ed., 1636-1638.

Nashville, TN: Thomas Nelson.

McEachern, W.A. (2012). Public goods and public choice. *Economics: A Contemporary*

Introduction, 353-367. Australia: Cengage Learning.

McGrath, R.J., Cumming, G.E., & Lasher, M.P. (2012). SOTIPS: Sex Offender Treatment

Intervention and Progress Scale. Retrieved from National Institute of Justice Website:

http://www.nij.gov/funding/2012/sotips-manual.pdf

Miller, J.A. (2010, December). Sex offender civil commitment: The treatment paradox.

California Law Review, 98(6), 2093-2121. Retrieved from Ebscohost.

More than Dillinger: Correctional records at the Indiana state archives. (2012). Retrieved from

the Friends of the Indiana State Archives Website: http://www.fisa-

in.org/news/articles/correctional.html

Nally, J., Lockwood, S., & Ho, T. (2012). The impact of education and employment on

recidivism. Retrieved from Indiana Department of Corrections Website:

http://www.in.gov/idoc/files/Impact_of_Education_and_Employment_on_Recidivism.pd

f

Nally, J., Lockwood, S., Ho, T., & Knutson, K. (2012, Spring). The post-release employment

and recidivism among different types of offenders with a different level of education: A

5-year follow-up study in Indiana. Retrieved from Center on Juvenile and Criminal

Justice Website: http://www.cjcj.org/files/The_Post-Release.pdf

Nelson, J. (2011, July). Statute requires SVP registration. *Indiana Lawyer*, 22(9), 23. Retrieved

from Ebscohost.

(the facility). (2012). Retrieved from (the corporation) Website: http://the(the

corporation)groupinc.com/Maps/LocationDetails/11

Offender Population Statistical Report. (2011, December). Published by the Indiana Department

of Correction Division of Research and Planning.

Overview of adult and juvenile facilities. (2012). Retrieved from Indiana Department of

Corrections Website: http://www.in.gov/idoc/2809.htm

Paparozzi, M.A. & Guy, R. (2009, November). The giant that never woke. *Journal of

Contemporary Criminal Justice*, 25(4), 397-411. Retrieved from Ebscohost.

Parole historical roots. (2012). Retrieved from the American Parole and Probation Association

Website: http://www.appa-net.org/eweb/Resources/PPCSW_10/historyparole.htm

Paul, R. & Elder, L. (2006). Deal with your irrational mind. *Critical Thinking: Learn the Tools

the Best Thinkers Use,* 213-255. Upper Saddle River, NJ: Pearson Prentice Hall.

Prescott, J.J. (2012, Summer). Do sex offender registries make us less safe? *Regulation*, 35(2), 48-55. Retrieved from Ebscohost.

Prescott, J.J. & Rockoff, J.E. (2011, February). Do sex offender registration and notification laws affect criminal behavior? *Journal of Law & Economics*, 54(1), 161-206. Retrieved from Ebscohost.

Robbins, S.P. & Judge, T.A. (2010). Power and politics. *Essentials of Organizational Behavior*, 181-193. Upper Saddle River, NJ: Prentice Hall.

Rudes, D.S. (2012, January). Framing organizational reform: Misalignments and disputes among parole and union middle managers. *Law & Policy*, 34(1), 1-31. DOI:10.1111/j.1467-9930.2011.00355.x.

Sex Offender Registries and Notification Programs. (2009, May). Retrieved from the University of Alaska Anchorage Justice Center Website: http://justice.uaa.alaska.edu/overview/2009/04.sex-offender-registries.pdf

Sex Offender Registration and Notification in the United States: Current Case Law and Issues. (2012, July). Retrieved from U.S. Department of Justice, Office of Sex Offender Sentencing, Monitoring, Apprehending, Registering, and Tracking (SMART): http://www.smart.gov/caselaw/handbook_july2012.pdf

Sex & Violent Offender Registry. (2012). Retrieved from Indiana Government Website: http://www.in.gov/idoc/reentry/2505.htm

Sex & Violent Offender Registration Responsibilities and Other Duties. (2012). Retrieved from IDOC Website: http://www.in.gov/idoc/reentry/files/Notification_Form_--_Duties_-_070108.pdf

Smith, P. & Schweitzer, M. (2012, February). The therapeutic prison. *Journal of Contemporary Criminal Justice*, 28(1), 7-22. DOI:10.1177/1043986211432201.

Spector, B. (2010). Mutual engagement and shared diagnosis. *Implementing Organizational Change: Theory Into Practice*, 2nd ed., 57-79. Upper Saddle River, NJ: Prentice Hall.

Spector, B. (2010). Organizational change. *Implementing Organizational Change: Theory Into Practice*, 2nd ed., 1-22. Upper Saddle River, NJ: Prentice Hall.

Spector, B. (2010). Theories of effective change implementation. *Implementing Organizational Change: Theory Into Practice*, 2nd ed., 24-55. Upper Saddle River, NJ: Prentice Hall.

Stafford, D. (2012, September). Sex offender registry listings subject of court appeals. *Indiana Lawyer,* 23(14), 3-18. Retrieved from Ebscohost.

STATIC-99/STATIC-99R. (2012). Retrieved from the Static 99 Website: http://www.static99.org/

Tewksberry, R., Jennings, W.G., & Zgoba, K. (2012, March). Sex offenders: Recidivism and Collateral Consequences. Retrieved from National Criminal Justice Research Services Website: https://www.ncjrs.gov/pdffiles1/nij/grants/238060.pdf

The Comprehensive Assessment Protocol: A System wide Review of Adult and Juvenile Sex Offender Management Strategies. (2007, July). Retrieved from Center for Sex Offender Management Website: http://www.csom.org/pubs/cap/download/Comprehensive%20Assessment%20Protocol.pdf

Thigpen, M.L., Beauclair, T.J., Keiser, G.M., & Banks, C. (2011, August). Special challenges facing parole. Retrieved from U.S. Department of Justice: National Institute of Corrections Website: http://nicic.gov/Library/024200

Tracking sex offenders with electronic monitoring technology: Implications and practical uses
for law enforcement. (2008, August). *International Association of Police Chiefs.*
Retrieved from Bureau of Justice Assistance Website:
https://www.bja.gov/Publications/IACPSexOffenderElecMonitoring.pdf

Twenty Strategies for Advancing Sex Offender Management in Your Jurisdiction. (2008,
December). Retrieved from Center for Sex Offender Management Website:
http://www.csom.org/pubs/twenty_strategies.pdf

Vrieze, S.I. & Grove, W.M. (2008, June). Predicting sex offender recidivism. I. Correcting for
item overselection and accuracy overestimation in scale development. II. Sampling error-
induced attenuation of predictive validity over base rate information. *Law & Human
Behavior*, 32(3), 266-278. DOI: 10.1007/s10979-007-9092-x.

Walters, G. (2011, June). Predicting recidivism with the psychological inventory of criminal
thinking styles and level of service inventory-revised: Screening version. *Law & Human
Behavior*, 35(3), 211-220. DOI:10.1007/s10979-010-9231-7.

Zgoba, K., Witt, P., Dalessandro, M., & Veysey, B. (2008, December). Megan's Law: Assessing
the Practical and Monetary Efficacy. *U.S. Department of Justice.* Retrieved from the
National Criminal Justice Reference Service Website:
https://www.ncjrs.gov/pdffiles1/nij/grants/225370.pdf

APPENDIX A[5]

Summaries of CSOM Handbooks for Policymakers and Practitioners and Sex Offender Management Strategies

Figure A1 - *Summary of Handbook Procedures for Policymaking*

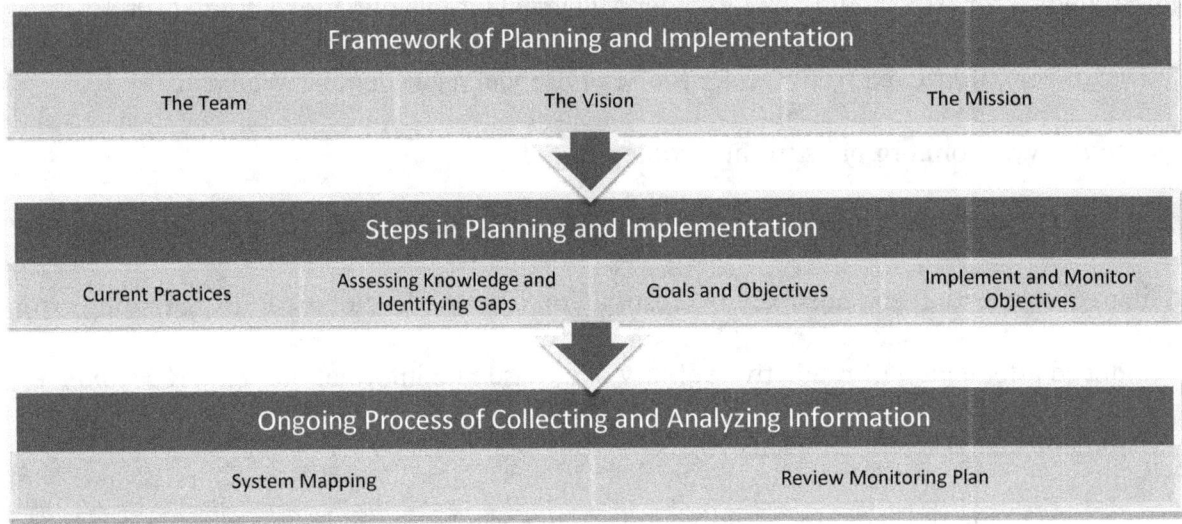

Figure A2 - *Summary of Approach to Management Strategies*

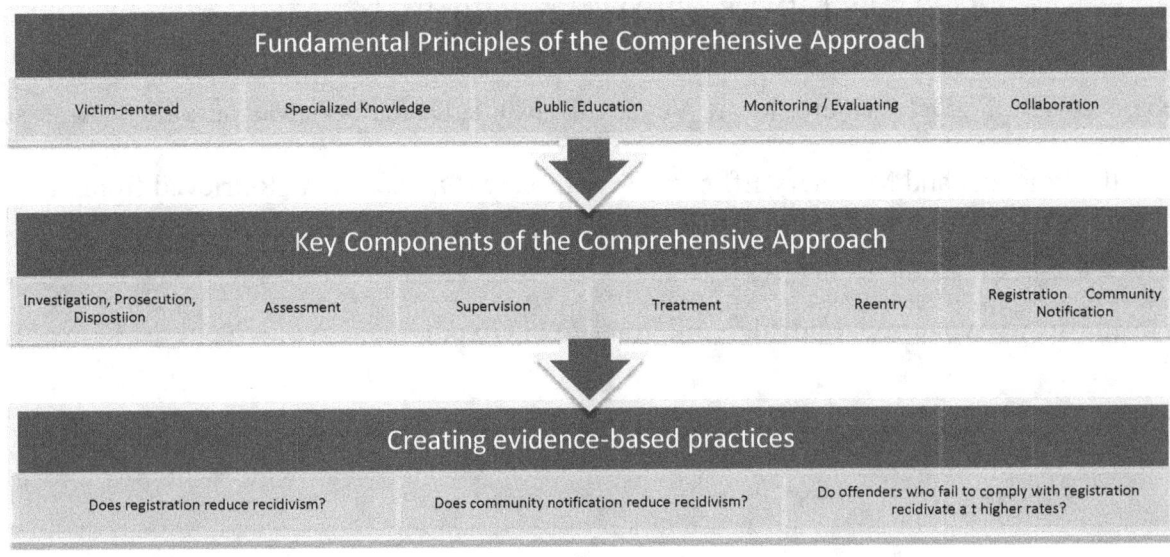

[5] Retrieved from Enhancing the Management of Adult and Juvenile Sex Offenders: A Handbook for Policymakers and Practitioners along with The Comprehensive Assessment Protocol: A Systemwide Review of Adult and Juvenile Sex Offender Management Strategies published by the Center for Sex Offender Management.

APPENDIX B[6]

IDOC Total Number of Sexual Offense Felonies
Committed to the Indiana Department of Corrections
Fiscal Year 2011

Figure B1 - *Summary Table of Felony Sexual Offenses*

OFFENSE – Citation Code	Female	Male
CLASS A OFFENSES:		
Attempt to Commit a Felony (35-41-2-4) Child Molesting	0	2
Child Molesting (35-42-2-1(5))	7	236
Conspiracy (35-41-5-2) Child Molesting	0	1
Rape (35-42-4-1)	0	30
Sexual Misconduct with a Minor (35-42-4-9)	0	1
CLASS B OFFENSES:		

Attempt to Commit a Felony (35-4-5-1)
    Child Molesting
    Criminal Deviate Conduct
    Rape
    Sexual Misconduct with a Minor
	0
	0
	0
	0
		1
		2
		3
		3

Child Molesting (35-42-4-3)	6	335
Child Solicitation	0	1
Incest (35-46-1-3)	0	16
Promoting Prostitution, under 18 (35-45-4-4)	1	2
Rape (35-42-4-1)	1	111
Sexual Misconduct with a Minor (35-42-4-9)	6	218
CLASS C OFFENSES:		
Aiding, Inducing, or Causing an Offense (35-41-2-4) Sexual Misconduct with a Minor		1
Attempt to Commit a Felony (35-41-5-1) Rape		1
Child Exploitation (35-42-4-4)	1	31
Child Molestation (35-42-4-3)	2	449
Child Solicitation (35-42-4-6)	0	26
Failure to Register as a Sex Offender (5-2-12-9)	1	129
Incest (35-46-1-3)	1	17
Sexual Battery (35-42-4-8)	0	2
Sexual Misconduct with a Minor (35-42-4-9)	8	204
Vicarious Sexual Gratification (35-42-4-5)	0	4

---

[6] Retrieved from Offender Population Statistical Report December 2011 published by Indiana Department of Correction Division of Research and Planning

CLASS D OFFENSES:

Attempt to Commit a Felony (35-41-5-1) Sexual Misconduct	0	1
Child Exploitation (35-42-4-3)	0	34
Child Molesting (35-4-4-3)	0	3
Child Pornography (35-42-4-4)	0	8
Child Seduction (35-42-4-7)	0	10
Child Solicitation (35-42-4-6)	0	25
Failure to Register as a Sex Offender (5-2-12-9)	2	244
Incest (35-46-1-3)	1	1
Prostitution (35-45-4-2)	36	6
Public Indecency (35-45-4-1)	3	9
Sexual Battery (35-42-4-8)	3	102
Sexual Misconduct (35-44-1-5)	1	4
Sexual Misconduct with a Minor (35-42-4-9)	2	37
Sex Offender Residency Restrictions (35-42-4-11)	0	16
Vicarious Sexual Gratification (35-42-4-5)	0	8
Voyeurism (35-45-4-5)	0	17
TOTAL OFFENSES:	75	2351

APPENDIX C[7]

IRAS-PIT (SAMPLE)

1.0 CRIMINAL HISTORY

    1.1 Most Serious Arrest Under Age 18

        0 = None

        1 = Yes, Misdemeanor

        2 = Yes, Felony

    1.2 Prior Commitment as Juvenile to Department of Youth Services

        (scoring and more items following)

2.0 SCHOOL BEHAVIOR AND EMPLOYMENT

3.0 FAMILY AND SOCIAL SUPPORT

4.0 SUBSTANCE ABUSE AND MENTAL HEALTH

5.0 CRIMINAL LIFESTYLE

PROFESSIONAL OVERRIDE (auxiliary)

IRAS-RT (SAMPLE)

1.0 CRIMINAL HISTORY

2.0 SOCIAL BONDS

    2.1 Ever Suspended or Expelled from School

        0 = No

        1 = Yes

    (scoring and more items following)

3.0 CRIMINAL ATTITUDES AND BEHAVIORAL PATTERNS

PROFESSIONAL OVERRIDE – includes reason for override, final level, recommendation, and a detailed list of Other Areas of Concern.

Other Areas of Concern

Low Intelligence*	Language
Physical Handicap	Ethnicity
Reading and Writing Limitations*	Cultural Barriers
Mental Health Issues*	History of Abuse / Neglect
No Desire to Change / Participate in Programs*	Interpersonal Anxiety
Transportation	Other (describe)
Child Care	*Recommendations for further assessment

APPENDIX D

---

[7] Retrieved from Indiana Risk Assessment Tool published by University of Cincinnati

APPENDIX D[8]

STATIC-99R

Static-99R Coding Form Question Number	Risk Factor	Codes		Score
1	Age at release	Aged 18 to 34.9 Aged 35 to 39.9 Aged 40 to 59.9 Aged 60 or older		1 0 -1 -3
2	Ever Lived With	Ever lived with lover for at least two years? Yes No		0 1
3	Index non-sexual violence - Any Convictions	No Yes		0 1
4	Prior non-sexual violence - Any Convictions	No Yes		0 1
5	Prior Sex Offences	Charges 0 1,2 3-5 6+	Convictions 0 1 2,3 4+	0 1 2 3
6	Prior sentencing dates (excluding index)	3 or less 4 or more		0 1
7	Any convictions for non-contact sex offences	No Yes		0 1
8	Any Unrelated Victims	No Yes		0 1
9	Any Stranger Victims	No Yes		0 1
10	Any Male Victims	No Yes		0 1
Total Score		**Add up scores from individual risk factors**		

Contact Information for the Author

---

[8] Retrieved from STATIC-99 Clearinghouse published by the same.

Dr. Kathy E. Williams

Lkone49kw@yahoo.com

Facebook, Twitter, and LinkedIn.

www.ingramcontent.com/pod-product-compliance
Lightning Source LLC
Chambersburg PA
CBHW081211180526
45170CB00006B/2305